PRAISE FOR *BUILDING A STORYBRAND*

"This is a seminal book built around an idea that will clarify, energize, and transform your business. Donald Miller offers a specific, detailed, and useful way to change the way you talk about the work you care about."

—SETH GODIN, AUTHOR OF *ALL MARKETERS ARE LIARS*

"Donald Miller ought to be working with your company just like he worked with ours. We changed our website after learning his framework and the results were fantastic. We noticed a difference right away. The StoryBrand Framework works—and we are implementing it companywide. Read this book!"

—KEN BLANCHARD, CHIEF SPIRITUAL OFFICER OF
THE KEN BLANCHARD COMPANIES AND COAUTHOR
OF *THE NEW ONE MINUTE MANAGER*®

"Donald Miller will teach you a lot more than how to sell products; he will teach you how to transform the lives of your customers. Your customers need you to play a role in their lives, and this book will teach you how. If you want your business to grow, read this book."

—JOHN C. MAXWELL, #1 *NEW YORK TIMES* BESTSELLING AUTHOR

"This is the most important business/marketing book of the year. All communicators know the power of Story. Donald Miller has captured the process to make your marketing pierce the white noise of the most overserved marketing generation in history. You *have* to read this book!"

—DAVE RAMSEY, #1 *NEW YORK TIMES* BESTSELLI

"Donald Miller reminds us that all good messaging begins with empathy. He knows that if you want to be seen, heard, a stood, the first step is to listen. Get this book if you want t with people in a profound way."

—BILL HASLAM, FORTY-NINTH GOVERNOR OF TE

"If you like making money, read this book. The StoryBrand Framework will help you create sales messages that people listen and respond to. We use it all the time and it works!"

—RYAN DEISS, FOUNDER AND CEO OF DIGITALMARKETER

"In only a few hours this book demystified lessons about branding that I've spent my entire career trying to understand. The brilliant StoryBrand Framework has now become the playbook for everything we do that is marketing-related."

—RORY VADEN, COFOUNDER OF SOUTHWESTERN CONSULTING AND *NEW YORK TIMES* BESTSELLING AUTHOR OF *TAKE THE STAIRS*

"I've been using Don Miller's StoryBrand framework in my business for a few years now. It's the single best marketing tool I know. We use it on every product we launch. I've had Don personally teach my company and clients and I recommend him to everyone. Now, all these revolutionary insights are easily accessible between these covers."

—MICHAEL HYATT, *NEW YORK TIMES* BESTSELLING AUTHOR OF *PLATFORM: GET NOTICED IN A NOISY WORLD*

BUILDING A STORYBRAND

Clarify Your Message So
Customers Will Listen

DONALD MILLER

HarperCollins
Leadership

An Imprint of HarperCollins

© 2017 by Donald Miller

Published by HarperCollins Leadership, an imprint of HarperCollins.

The author is represented by Ambassador Literary Agency, Nashville, TN.

Graphics designed by Kyle Reid.

ISBN 978-0-7180-3333-0 (eBook)

ISBN 978-1-4002-0183-9 (IE)

Library of Congress Control Number: 2017937432
ISBN 978-0-7180-3332-3

Printed in the United States of America

20 21 LSC 20 19

This book is dedicated to:
Tim Schurrer and Kyle Reid
for believing in the framework from the beginning.
What I love most about StoryBrand is it
allowed us to become friends.

And also:
Betsy Miller
Avery Csorba
Koula Callahan
JJ Peterson
Chad Snavely
Suzanne Norman
You are living proof that when a group of friends sacrifice
together for a common good, they can become family.

CONTENTS

SECTION 3: IMPLEMENTING YOUR STORYBRAND BRANDSCRIPT

INTRODUCTION

This is not a book about telling your company's story. A book like that would be a waste of time. Customers don't generally care about your story; they care about their own.

Your customer should be the hero of the story, not your brand. This is the secret every phenomenally successful business understands.

What follows is a seven-part framework that will change the way you talk about your business and perhaps the way you *do* business.

Each year we help more than three thousand businesses stop wasting money on marketing and get their company growing by helping them clarify their message. This framework will work for you, regardless of your industry.

To get the most out of this book, I encourage you to do three things:

1. Read the book and understand the SB7 Framework.
2. Filter your message through the framework.
3. Clarify your message so more customers listen.

Marketing has changed. Businesses that invite their customers into a heroic story grow. Businesses that don't are forgotten.

May we all be richly rewarded for putting our customers' stories above our own.

WHY MOST MARKETING IS A MONEY PIT

CHAPTER 1

THE KEY TO BEING SEEN, HEARD, AND UNDERSTOOD

Most companies waste enormous amounts of money on marketing. We all know how mind-numbing it is to spend precious dollars on a new marketing effort that gets no results. When we see the reports, we wonder what went wrong, or worse, whether our product is really as good as we thought it was.

But what if the problem wasn't the product? What if the problem was the way we talked about the product?

The problem is simple. The graphic artists and designers we're hiring to build our websites and brochures have degrees in design and know everything about Photoshop, but how many of them have read a single book about writing good sales copy? How many of them know how to clarify your message so customers listen? And worse, these companies are glad to take your money, regardless of whether you see results or not.

The fact is, pretty websites don't sell things. Words sell things. And if we haven't clarified our message, our customers won't listen.

If we pay a lot of money to a design agency without first clarifying our message, we might as well be holding a bullhorn up to a monkey. The only thing a potential customer will hear is noise.

Still, clarifying our message isn't easy. I had one client say that when he tried to do so, he felt like he was inside the bottle trying to read the label. I understand. Before I started StoryBrand I was a writer and spent thousands of hours staring at a blank computer screen, wondering what to say. That soul-wrenching frustration led me to create a "communication framework" based on the proven power of story, and I swear it was like discovering a secret formula. The writing got easier and I sold millions of books. After using the framework to create clear messages in my books, I used it to filter the marketing collateral in my own small company. Once we got clear, we doubled in revenue for four consecutive years. I now teach that framework to more than three thousand businesses each year.

Once they get their message straight, our clients create quality websites, incredible keynotes, e-mails that get opened, and sales letters people respond to. Why? Because nobody will listen to you if your message isn't clear, no matter how expensive your marketing material may be.

At StoryBrand we've had clients double, triple, and even quadruple their revenue after they got one thing straight—their message.

The StoryBrand Framework has been just as effective for billion-dollar brands as it has for mom-and-pop businesses, and just as powerful for American corporations as it has for those in Japan and Africa. Why? Because the human brain, no matter what region of the world it comes from, is drawn toward clarity and away from confusion.

The reality is we aren't just in a race to get our products to market; we're also in a race to communicate why our customers need those products in their lives. Even if we have the best product in the marketplace, we'll lose to an inferior product if our competitor's offer is communicated more clearly.

So what's your message? Can you say it easily? Is it simple, relevant, and repeatable? Can your entire team repeat your company's message in such a way that it is compelling? Have new hires been given talking points they can use to describe what the company offers and why every potential customer should buy it?

How many sales are we missing out on because customers can't figure out what our offer is within five seconds of visiting our website?

WHY SO MANY BUSINESSES FAIL

To find out why so many marketing and branding attempts fail, I called my friend Mike McHargue. Mike, often called "Science Mike" because he hosts a successful podcast called *Ask Science Mike*, spent fifteen years using science-based methodologies to help companies figure out how their customers think, specifically in the tech space. Sadly, he left advertising when a client asked him to create an algorithm predicting the associated buying habits of people with diabetes. Translation: they wanted him to sell junk food to diabetics. Mike refused and left the industry. He's a good man. I called, though, because he still has incredible insight as to how marketing, story, and behavior all blend together.

At my request, Mike flew to Nashville to attend one of our workshops. After two days learning the StoryBrand 7-Part Framework (hereafter called the SB7 Framework), we sat on my back porch and I grilled him with questions. Why does this formula work? What's happening in the brains of consumers as they encounter a message filtered through this formula? What's the science behind why brands like Apple and Coke, who intuitively use this formula, dominate the marketplace?

"There's a reason most marketing collateral doesn't work," Mike said, putting his feet up on the coffee table. "Their marketing is too complicated. The brain doesn't know how to process the information. The more simple and predictable the communication, the easier it is for the brain to digest. Story helps because it is a sense-making mechanism. Essentially, story formulas put everything in order so the brain doesn't have to work to understand what's going on."

Mike went on to explain that among the million things the brain is good at, the overriding function of the brain is to help an individual survive and thrive. Everything the human brain does, all day, involves helping that person, and the people that person cares about, get ahead in life.

Mike asked if I remembered that old pyramid we learned about in high school, Abraham Maslow's hierarchy of needs. First, he reminded me, the brain is tasked with setting up a system in which we can eat and drink and survive physically. In our modern, first-world economy this means having a job and a dependable income. Then the brain is concerned with safety, which might entail having a roof over our heads and a sense of well-being and power that keeps us from being vulnerable. After food and shelter are taken care of, our brains start thinking about our relationships, which entail everything from reproducing in a sexual relationship, to being nurtured in a romantic relationship, to creating friendships (a tribe) who will stick by us in case there are any social threats. Finally, the brain begins to concern itself with greater psychological, physiological, or even spiritual needs that give us a sense of meaning.

What Mike helped me understand is that, without us knowing it, human beings are constantly scanning their environment (even advertising) for information that is going to help them meet their primitive need to survive. This means that when we ramble on and on about how we have the biggest manufacturing plant on the West Coast, our customers don't care. Why? Because that information isn't helping them eat, drink, find a mate, fall in love, build a tribe, experience a deeper sense of meaning, or stockpile weapons in case barbarians start coming over the hill behind our cul-de-sac.

So what do customers do when we blast a bunch of noise at them? They ignore us.

And so right there on my back porch, Mike defined two critical mistakes brands make when they talk about their products and services.

Mistake Number One

The first mistake brands make is they fail to focus on the aspects of their offer that will help people survive and thrive.

All great stories are about survival—either physical, emotional, relational, or spiritual. A story about anything else won't work to captivate an audience. Nobody's interested. This means that if we position our products and services as anything but an aid in helping people survive, thrive, be accepted, find love, achieve an aspirational identity, or bond with a tribe that will defend them physically and socially, good luck selling anything to anybody. These are the only things people care about. We can take that truth to the bank. Or to bankruptcy court, should we choose to ignore it as an undeniable fact.

Mike said our brains are constantly sorting through information and so we discard millions of unnecessary facts every day. If we were to spend an hour in a giant ballroom, our brains would never think to count how many chairs are in the room. Meanwhile, we would always know where the exits are. Why? Because our brains don't need to know how many chairs there are in the room to survive, but knowing where the exits are would be helpful in case there was a fire.

Without knowing it, the subconscious is always categorizing and organizing information, and when we talk publicly about our company's random backstory or internal goals, we're positioning ourselves as the chairs, not the exits.

"But this poses a problem," Mike continued. "Processing information demands that the brain burn calories. And the burning of too many calories acts against the brain's primary job: to help us survive and thrive."

Mistake Number Two

The second mistake brands make is they cause their customers to burn too many calories in an effort to understand their offer.

When having to process too much seemingly random

information, people begin to ignore the source of that useless information in an effort to conserve calories. In other words, there's a survival mechanism within our customers' brain that is designed to tune us out should we ever start confusing them.

Imagine every time we talk about our products to potential customers, they have to start running on a treadmill. Literally, they have to jog the whole time we're talking. How long do you think they're going to pay attention? Not long. And yet this is precisely what's happening. When we start our elevator pitch or keynote address, or when somebody visits our website, they're burning calories to process the information we're sharing. And if we don't say something (and say something quickly) they can use to survive or thrive, they will tune us out.

These two realities—the reality that people are looking for brands that can help them survive and thrive, and the reality that communication must be simple—explain why the SB7 Framework has helped so many businesses increase their revenue. The key is to make your company's message about something that helps the customer survive and to do so in such a way that they can understand it without burning too many calories.

STORY TO THE RESCUE

Mike agreed the most powerful tool we can use to organize information so people don't have to burn very many calories is story. As he said, story is a sense-making device. It identifies a necessary ambition, defines challenges that are battling to keep us from achieving that ambition, and provides a plan to help us conquer those challenges. When we define the elements of a story as it relates to our brand, we create a map customers can follow to engage our products and services.

Still, when I talk about story to business leaders, they immediately put me in a category with artists, thinking I want to introduce them to something fanciful. But that's not what I'm talking about. I'm talking about a concrete formula we can use to garner attention from otherwise distracted customers. I'm talking about practical steps we can take to make sure people see us, hear us, and understand exactly why they simply *must* engage our products.

THE FORMULA FOR CLEAR COMMUNICATION

Formulas are simply the summation of best practices, and the reason we like them is because they work. We've been given great management formulas like Ken Blanchard's Situational Leadership and formulas we can use in manufacturing like Six Sigma and Lean Manufacturing. But what about a formula for communication? Why don't we have a formula we can use to effectively explain what our company offers the world?

The StoryBrand Framework is that formula. We know it works because some form of this formula has been active for thousands of years to help people tell stories. Talk about a summation of best practices. When it comes to getting people to pay attention, this formula will be your most powerful ally.

Once you know the formulas, you can predict the path most stories will take. I've learned these formulas so well that my wife hates going to movies with me because she knows at some point

I'm going to elbow her and whisper something like, "That guy s going to die in thirty-one minutes."

Story formulas reveal a well-worn path in the human brain, and if we want to stay in business, we need to position our products along this path.

If you're going to continue reading this book, I have to warn you, I'm going to ruin movies for you. I mean, these things really are formulaic. They're predictable. And they're predictable for a reason. Storytellers have figured out how to keep an audience's attention for hours.

The good news is these formulas work just as well at growing your business as they do at entertaining an audience.

THE KEY IS CLARITY

The narrative coming out of a company (and for that matter inside a company) must be clear. In a story, audiences must always know who the hero is, what the hero wants, who the hero has to defeat to get what they want, what tragic thing will happen if the hero doesn't win, and what wonderful thing will happen if they do. If an audience can't answer these basic questions, they'll check out and the movie will lose millions at the box office. If a screenwriter breaks these rules, they'll likely never work again.

The same is true for the brand you represent. Our customers have questions burning inside them, and if we aren't answering those questions, they'll move on to another brand. If we haven't identified what our customer wants, what problem we are helping them solve, and what life will look like after they engage our products and services, for example, we can forget about thriving in the marketplace. Whether we're writing a story or attempting to sell products, our message must be clear. Always.

In fact, at StoryBrand we have a mantra: "If you confuse, you'll lose."

BUSINESS HAS AN ENEMY

Business has a fierce, insidious enemy that, if not identified and combated, will contort our company into an unrecognizable mess. The enemy I'm talking about is noise.

Noise has killed more ideas, products, and services than taxes, recessions, lawsuits, climbing interest rates, and even inferior product design. I'm not talking about the noise inside our business; I'm talking about the noise we *create* as a business. What we often call marketing is really just clutter and confusion sprayed all over our websites, e-mails, and commercials. And it's costing us millions.

Years ago, a StoryBrand client who attended one of our workshops pushed back. "I don't think this will work for me," he said. "My business is too diverse to reduce down to a simple message." I asked him to explain.

"I have an industrial painting company with three different revenue streams. In one division we powder-coat auto parts. In another we apply sealant to concrete, and in another we have a sterilized painting process used specifically in hospitals."

His business was diverse, but nothing so complex that it couldn't be simplified so more people would hire him. I asked if I could put his website on the giant television screen so the entire workshop could see it. His website was thoughtful, but it didn't make a great deal of sense from an outside perspective (which is how every customer views your business).

The man had hired a fine-arts painter to create a painting of his building (was he selling a building?), and at first glance it looked like the website for an Italian restaurant. The first question I had when I went to the website was, "Do you serve free breadsticks?" There were a thousand links ranging from contact information to FAQs to a timeline of the company's history. There were even links to the nonprofits the business supported. It was as though he was answering a hundred questions his customers had never asked.

I asked the class to raise their hands if they thought his business would grow if we wiped the website clean and simply featured an image of a guy in a white lab coat painting something next to text that read, "We Paint All Kinds of S#*%," accompanied by a button in the middle of the page that said, "Get a Quote."

The entire class raised their hands.

Of course his business would grow. Why? Because he'd finally stopped forcing clients to burn calories thinking about his life and business and offered the one thing that would solve his customers' problem: a painter.

What we think we are saying to our customers and what our customers actually hear are two different things. And customers make buying decisions not based on what we say but on what they hear.

STOP SAYING THAT

All experienced writers know the key to great writing isn't in what they say; it's in what they don't say. The more we cut out, the better the screenplay or book. The mathematician and philosopher Blaise Pascal is often credited for sending a long letter stating he simply didn't have time to send a short one.

If we want to connect with customers, we have to stop blasting them with noise.

The beautiful thing about clarifying our message using the SB7 Framework is it makes communicating easy. No longer will you sit in front of a blank page wondering what to say on your website, in your elevator pitch, in your e-mail blast, in your Facebook ads, or even on your television or radio commercials.

CLARIFY YOUR MESSAGE

Whether we run a small company or a multibillion-dollar brand, confusing our customers is costing us money. How many of our team members can't explain how we help our customers survive and thrive? How many people are buying from our competition because they've communicated more clearly than we have? How long will we last if we keep talking about aspects of our products our customers don't care about?

Things can be different.

To clarify our message we're going to need a formula. A serious formula. This formula needs to organize our thinking, reduce our marketing effort, obliterate confusion, terrify the competition, and finally get our businesses growing again.

Let's learn about that formula now.

—— CHAPTER 2 ——

THE SECRET WEAPON THAT WILL GROW YOUR BUSINESS

To help you grow your company, I'm going to guide you in simplifying your message into soundbites that come from seven categories. Once you have these seven messages down, any anxiety you experience talking about your brand will subside and customers will be more attracted to what you offer. We are going to figure out your customers' story and place ourselves right smack in the middle of it.

Story is atomic. It is perpetual energy and can power a city. Story is the one thing that can hold a human being's attention for hours.

Nobody can look away from a good story. In fact, neuroscientists claim the average human being spends more than 30 percent of their time daydreaming . . . *unless* they're reading, listening to, or watching a story unfold. Why? Because when we are engaged in a story, the story does the daydreaming for us.

Story is the greatest weapon we have to combat noise, because it organizes information in such a way that people are compelled to listen.

STORY MAKES MUSIC OUT OF NOISE

Living in Nashville I've learned quite a bit about the difference between music and noise. Nearly half our friends here are musicians. I'm always amazed at their talent. Hardly a dinner party goes by without somebody grabbing a guitar.

I could summarize what I've learned about the difference between music and noise by saying my friends make music and I make noise, but there's actually some complicated science involved.

Technically speaking, music and noise are similar. Both are created by traveling sound waves that rattle our eardrums. Music, however, is noise that has been submitted to certain rules that allow the brain to engage on a different level. If I played you a recording of a dump truck backing up, birds chirping, and children laughing, you'd not remember those sounds the next day. But if I played you a Beatles song, you'd likely be humming it for a week.

There is an obvious difference between a well-choreographed piece of music and the sound of a cat chasing a rat through a wind-chime factory, which is the equivalent of the average corporate website, keynote speech, or elevator pitch.

The brain remembers music and forgets about noise just like the brain remembers some brands and forgets about others.

Story is similar to music. A good story takes a series of random events and distills them into the essence of what really matters. There's a reason the final cut of a movie is called a final cut. Prior to the theatrical version, a film has gone through rounds upon rounds of edits, omissions, revisions, and deletions. Sometimes entire characters end up on the cutting-room floor. Why? Because storytellers have filters to cut out the noise. If a character or scene doesn't serve the plot, it has to go.

When clients want to add a bunch of confusion to their marketing message, I ask them to consider the ramifications of doing so if they were writing a screenplay. I mean, what if *The Bourne Identity* were a movie about a spy named Jason Bourne searching for his true identity but it also included scenes of Bourne trying to lose weight, marry a girl, pass the bar exam, win on *Jeopardy*, and adopt a cat? The audience would lose interest. When storytellers bombard people with too much information, the audience is forced to burn too many calories organizing the data. As a result, they daydream, walk out of the theater, or in the case of digital marketing, click to another site without placing an order.

Why do so many brands create noise rather than music? It's because they don't realize they are creating noise. They actually think people are interested in the random information they're doling out.

This is why we need a filter. The essence of branding is to create simple, relevant messages we can repeat over and over so that we "brand" ourselves into the public consciousness.

STEVE JOBS AND THE
MESSAGE OF APPLE

Apple grew much larger only after Steve Jobs began filtering his message through the lens of story. Transformation in his thinking happened after working with (and partially creating) the genius storytelling factory that is Pixar. When Jobs came back to Apple after being surrounded by professional storytellers, he realized story was everything.

Just think about the incredible transformation that took place in Steve's life and career after Pixar. In 1983, Apple launched their computer Lisa, the last project Jobs worked on before he was let go. Jobs released Lisa with a nine-page ad in the *New York Times* spelling out the computer's technical features. It was nine pages of geek talk nobody outside NASA was interested in. The computer bombed.

When Jobs returned to the company after running Pixar, Apple became customer-centric, compelling, and clear in their communication. The first campaign he released went from nine pages in the *New York Times* to just two words on billboards all over America: *Think Different.*

When Apple began filtering their communication to make it simple and relevant, they actually stopped featuring computers in most of their advertising. Instead, they understood their customers were all living, breathing heroes, and they tapped into their stories. They did this by (1) identifying what their customers wanted (to be seen and heard), (2) defining their customers' challenge (that people didn't recognize their hidden genius), and (3) offering their customers a tool they could use to express themselves (computers and smartphones). Each of these realizations are pillars in ancient storytelling and critical for connecting with customers.

I'll teach you about these three pillars and more in the coming chapters, but for now just realize the time Apple spent clarifying the role they play in their customers' story is one of the primary factors responsible for their growth.

Notice, though, the story of Apple isn't about Apple; it's about you. You're the hero in the story, and they play a role more like Q in the James Bond movies. They are the guy you go see when you need a tool to help you win the day.

Despite what acolytes of the cult of Mac may say, Apple likely doesn't make the best computers or phones. "Best" is subjective, of course. Whether Apple has the best technology, though, is debatable.

But it doesn't matter. People don't buy the best products; they buy the products they can understand the fastest. Apple has inserted themselves into their customers' story like no other technology company, and as a result, they're not only the largest technology company, they're in the top ten largest companies period.[1] If we want our companies to grow, we should borrow a page from their playbook. We should clarify our message.

STORY CAN GROW YOUR BUSINESS

To better understand what Steve Jobs learned during his days at Pixar, let's take off our business hats for a few pages and pretend we're learning about story for the first time. Once you understand how story integrates with your brand message, you'll be able to create communication pieces (and even a brand strategy) that engages more customers and grows your business. And if you really get this down, people around the office will wonder how in the world you became such a marketing genius.

After studying hundreds of movies, novels, plays, and musicals across nearly every imaginable genre, and after having written eight books of my own along with a nationally released screenplay, I've narrowed down the necessary elements of a compelling story to seven basic plot points. If we were writing a full screenplay, of course, we'd need more, but for purposes of understanding and entering into our customers' story, there are only seven.

Story in a Nutshell

Here is nearly every story you see or hear in a nutshell: A ① CHARACTER who wants something encounters a ② PROBLEM before they can get it. At the peak of their despair, a ③ GUIDE steps into their lives, gives them a ④ PLAN, and CALLS THEM TO ⑤ ACTION. That action helps them avoid ⑥ FAILURE and ends in a ⑦ SUCCESS.

That's really it. You'll see some form of this structure in nearly every movie you watch from here on out. These seven basic plot points are like chords of music in the sense that you can use them to create an infinite variety of narrative expression. Just like playing the guitar, with these seven chords you can create any number of songs. Varying too far from these chords, however, means you risk descending into noise.

Let's look at how this simple framework plays out in a couple of familiar stories. Once you can recognize the framework in stories, you'll start to understand exactly where the story of your brand is confusing customers by not sticking to the formula.

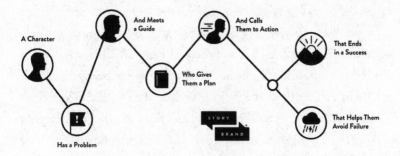

In the first *Hunger Games* movie, Katniss Everdeen must compete in a twisted fight-to-the-death tournament forced upon the people of Panem by an evil, tyrannical government called the Capitol. The problem she faces is obvious: she must kill or be killed. Katniss is overwhelmed, underprepared, and outnumbered.

Along comes Haymitch, the brash, liquor-loving, grizzled winner of a previous Hunger Games tournament. Haymitch assumes the role of Katniss's mentor, helping her hatch a plan to win over the public. This gains Katniss more sponsors, thereby equipping her with more resources for the fight and increasing her chances of winning.

Here is the first *Hunger Games* story laid out on the StoryBrand grid:

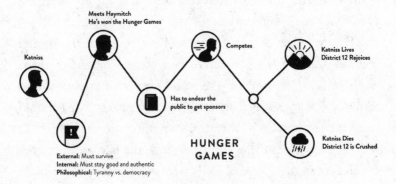

In *Star Wars: A New Hope*, our reluctant hero, Luke Skywalker, experiences a devastating tragedy: his aunt and uncle are murdered at the hands of the evil Empire. This sets a series of events in motion: Luke begins the journey of becoming a Jedi Knight and destroys the Empire's battle station, the Death Star, which allows the Rebellion to live and fight another day. Enter a guide, Obi-Wan Kenobi, a former Jedi Knight who once trained Luke's father.

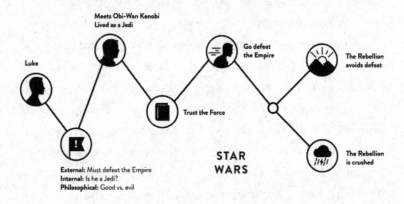

Not every story works this way, but most do. Sometimes a writer will bring in multiple guides or (usually to the story's peril) leave the guide out, but the formula holds up in almost every story you'll encounter.

The fact that nearly every movie you go see at the theater includes these seven elements means something. After thousands of years, storytellers the world over have arrived at this formula as a means of best practices. Simply put, this framework is the pinnacle of narrative communication. The further we veer away from these seven elements, the harder it becomes for audiences to engage. This is why indie films, which often break from the formula to gain critical acclaim, fail miserably at the box office. Critics are hungry for something different, yet the masses, who do not study movies professionally, simply want accessible stories.

It seems true that some brands (as well as some screenwriters) break these formulas and succeed all the same, but when you look closely, this is rarely the case. Truly creative and brilliant marketers and screenwriters know how to use the formula while still avoiding cliché. This, in my opinion, is what makes them brilliant. When you get good at the SB7 Framework, hardly anybody will notice you are using it.

The Three Crucial Questions

So how do we make the story our company is telling clear?

Remember, the greatest enemy our business faces is the same enemy that good stories face: noise. At no point should we be able to pause a movie and be unable to answer three questions:

1. What does the hero want?
2. Who or what is opposing the hero getting what she wants?
3. What will the hero's life look like if she does (or does not) get what she wants?

If you've ever started daydreaming in a movie, it was likely because you couldn't answer one of these three questions, or worse, you didn't care. Here's the kicker: if these three questions can't be answered within the first fifteen to twenty minutes, the story has already descended into noise and will almost certainly fail at the box office.

At StoryBrand our Certified Guides have reviewed thousands of pages of marketing copy that had nothing to do with the story of the customer. We tell our clients the same thing my filmmaker friends told me when I was writing screenplays: anything that doesn't serve the plot has to go. Just because a tagline sounds great or a picture on a website grabs the eye, that doesn't mean it helps us enter into our customers' story. In every line of copy we write, we're either serving the customer's story or descending into confusion; we're either making music or making noise.

Nobody remembers a company that makes noise.

DOES YOUR MARKETING PASS THE GRUNT TEST?

Just like there are three questions audiences must be able to answer to engage in a story, there are three questions potential customers must answer if we expect them to engage with our brand. And they should be able to answer these questions within five seconds of looking at our website or marketing material:

1. What do you offer?
2. How will it make my life better?
3. What do I need to do to buy it?

At StoryBrand we call this *passing the grunt test*. The critical question is this: "Could a caveman look at your website and immediately grunt what you offer?"

Imagine a guy wearing a bearskin T-shirt, sitting in a cave

by a fire, with a laptop across his lap. He's looking at your website. Would he be able to grunt an answer to the three questions posed above? If you were an aspirin company, would he be able to grunt, "You sell headache medicine, me feel better fast, me get it at Walgreens"? If not, you're likely losing sales.

CLARITY PRODUCES RESULTS

One of our early clients, Kyle Shultz, was a fireman in Ohio who looked into StoryBrand because he wanted to leave his job and pursue his passion of teaching photography. He had recently launched an online photography course aimed at parents. He'd worked hard to create terrific video training allowing moms everywhere to finally start using that basic camera they'd placed in the junk drawer because they felt it was too complicated. Interest was decent. In his first launch, he sold $25,000 worth of online courses. He was ecstatic. Still, it wasn't enough money for him to quit his job and pursue teaching photography full-time.

When Kyle subscribed to the *Building a StoryBrand* podcast, he began to wonder whether his message was too confusing. The night before his next launch he bought our online course and edited his website using the SB7 Framework. In fact, he removed 90 percent of the text he'd previously used on his sales page, and he also stopped using inside language like "f-stop" and "depth of field." Instead, he used phrases like "Take those great pictures where the background is blurry."

The next day Kyle sent a mass e-mail to the exact same e-mail list he'd contacted only six months before and offered the course again. He wasn't expecting much because he'd already sold to this list, but to his surprise the course sold another $103,000 worth of registrations.

The difference? He highlighted the aspects of his course that would help parents survive and thrive (build stronger tribes, strengthen family connections, and connect more deeply with life's greater meaning), and he did so in such a simple way (with fewer than three hundred words on his sales page) that people didn't have to burn calories to figure out what was in it for them. Overnight he'd gone from a cluttered mess to the clear guide in his customers' story.

Today, Kyle has quit his job and runs shultzphotoschool.com full-time. Every day he gets e-mails from parents thanking him for helping them feel great about the photographs they're taking of their children.

WE NEED A FILTER

Alfred Hitchcock defined a good story as "life with the dull parts taken out."[2] Good branding is the same. Our companies are complex, for sure, but a good messaging filter will remove all the stuff that bores our customers and will bear down on the aspects of our brand that will help them survive and thrive.

So how do we come up with these messages? It's simple. We use the same grid storytellers use in telling stories to map out the story of our customers, then we create clear and refined statements in the seven relevant categories of their lives to position ourselves as their guides. When we do this, we become the people who help them overcome their challenges and achieve the life they want to live.

Once we begin filtering our message through the SB7 Framework and using it as a communication filter, we will be able to repeat powerful messages over and over that "brand" us into our customers' story.

The SB7 Framework is simple, fun, and effective. And when you're done, your entire brand message is going to sit on a single sheet of paper. We call this single sheet of paper (actually, it's a free digital application I'm going to introduce you to) the StoryBrand BrandScript.

Once you've finished the process, you'll use your BrandScript to create all manner of improved marketing material, and you'll be more clearly positioned in the marketplace. When customers finally understand how you can help them live a wonderful story, your company will grow.

With that, let's take a look at the StoryBrand Framework.

CHAPTER 3

THE SIMPLE SB7 FRAMEWORK

In the next section of this book, I'll dive deep into the elements of the SB7 Framework, showing you how each important category of messaging makes your brand inviting to customers. For now, though, let's fly over the framework so you can understand, in summary form, all that it can do to simplify your marketing and messaging.

THE STORYBRAND FRAMEWORK

1. A Character

 STORYBRAND PRINCIPLE ONE: THE CUSTOMER IS THE HERO, NOT YOUR BRAND.

A major paradigm shift in the SB7 Framework is that the

customer is the hero of the story, not your brand. When we position our customer as the hero and ourselves as the guide, we will be recognized as a trusted resource to help them overcome their challenges.

Positioning the customer as the hero in the story is more than just good manners; it's also good business. Communication expert Nancy Duarte has done extensive research on how to create powerful presentations. The strategy she recommends to her clients is simple: when giving a speech, position yourself as Yoda and your audience as Luke Skywalker.[1] It's a small but powerful shift that honors the journey of the audience and positions us as a leader providing wisdom, products, and services our audience needs in order to thrive.

Once we identify who our customer is, we have to ask ourselves what they want as it relates to our brand. The catalyst for any story is that the hero wants something. The rest of the story is a journey about discovering whether the hero will get what they want.

Unless we identify something our customer wants, they will never feel invited into the story we are telling. As we explore the first element of the StoryBrand Framework, I'll show you why and how to invite customers into a story that makes them want to pay attention to your brand.

2. Has a Problem

STORYBRAND PRINCIPLE TWO: COMPANIES TEND TO SELL SOLUTIONS TO EXTERNAL PROBLEMS, BUT CUSTOMERS BUY SOLUTIONS TO INTERNAL PROBLEMS.

In its purest form, a story starts with a character who lives in peace and stability. Suddenly that stability is disrupted: a bomb goes off, someone is kidnapped, or a disaster strikes. The hero then sets out on a journey to return to the peaceful life they once enjoyed.

Customers are attracted to us for the same reason heroes are pulled into stories: they want to solve a problem that has, in big or small ways, disrupted their peaceful life. If we sell lawn-care products, they're coming to us because they're embarrassed about their lawn or they simply don't have time to do the work. If we sell financial advice, they're coming to us because they're worried about their retirement plan. It may not be as dramatic or sexy as James Bond going to Q to grab the latest high-tech spy weapons, but the premise is the same: our customers are in trouble and they need help.

By talking about the problems our customers face, we deepen their interest in everything we offer.

What most brands miss, however, is that there are three levels of problems a customer encounters. In stories, heroes encounter external, internal, and philosophical problems. Why? Because these are the same three levels of problems human beings face in their everyday lives. Almost all companies try to sell solutions to external problems, but as we unfold the StoryBrand Framework, you'll see why customers are much more motivated to resolve their inner frustrations.

In the second part of the StoryBrand Framework, we'll look at the three levels of problems our customers experience and create messages offering to resolve those problems. Understanding and addressing the three levels of problems our customers face will help us create a brand promise that will connect with customers on a primitive level and at their deepest point of need. This, in turn, will help us endear customers and create passionate brand evangelists.

3. And Meets a Guide

 StoryBrand Principle Three: Customers aren't looking for another hero; they're looking for a guide.

If heroes in a story could solve their own problems, they would never get into trouble in the first place. That's why storytellers, through the centuries, have created another character to help the hero win. Depending on the scholar you talk to, there are many names for this character, but the term we use at StoryBrand is *the guide*.

In Tom Hooper's Academy Award–winning film *The King's Speech*, King George VI struggles to overcome a stutter. As Britain prepares for war against Germany, the Brits look to their leader for confidence and direction. Desperate, King George VI solicits the help of Lionel Logue, a dramatist turned speech therapist, who gives him a plan, coaches him to competency, and helps him transform into a powerful orator. This is the same service Obi-Wan (and Yoda) offers Luke Skywalker in *Star Wars*, Haymitch offers Katniss in *The Hunger Games*, and, to some degree, Bing Bong offers Joy in Pixar's *Inside Out*.

It's no accident that guides show up in almost every movie. Nearly every human being is looking for a guide (or guides) to help them win the day.

Brands that position themselves as *heroes* unknowingly

compete with their potential customers. Every human being wakes up each morning and sees the world through the lens of a protagonist. The world revolves around us, regardless of how altruistic, generous, and selfless a person we may be. Each day is, quite literally, about how *we* encounter our world. Potential customers feel the same way about themselves. They are the center of their world.

When a brand comes along and positions itself as the hero, customers remain distant. They hear us talking about how great our business is and start wondering if we're competing with them for scarce resources. Their subconscious thought pattern goes like this: *Oh, this is another hero, like me. I wish I had more time to hear their story, but right now I'm busy looking for a guide.*

In the third part of the StoryBrand Framework, we'll look at two mental triggers that will help customers recognize us as the guide they've been looking for.

4. Who Gives Them a Plan

 STORYBRAND PRINCIPLE FOUR: CUSTOMERS TRUST A GUIDE WHO HAS A PLAN.

At this point we've identified what the customer wants, defined three levels of problems they're encountering, and positioned ourselves as their guide. And our customers love us for the effort. But they still aren't going to make a purchase. Why? Because we haven't laid out a simple plan of action they can take.

Making a purchase is a huge step, especially if our products or services are expensive. What customers are looking for, then, is a clear path we've laid out that takes away any confusion they might have about how to do business with us. The StoryBrand tool we will use to create this path is called *the plan*.

In almost every story, the guide gives the hero a plan, or a bit of information, or a few steps they can use to get the job done. In the *Star Wars* movies, Yoda tells Luke to trust the Force and then trains Luke on how to wield this power. People are looking for a philosophy they can embody or a series of steps they can take to solve their problems.

In the fourth part of the StoryBrand Framework, we'll look at two kinds of plans: the agreement plan and the process plan. Each of these plans will earn trust and offer our customers a clear path to stability, greatly increasing the chance they will make a purchase.

5. And Calls Them to Action

 STORYBRAND PRINCIPLE FIVE: CUSTOMERS DO NOT TAKE ACTION UNLESS THEY ARE CHALLENGED TO TAKE ACTION.

In stories, characters don't take action on their own. They must be challenged. If we're telling a story about a man who needs to lose thirty pounds and suddenly decides to do it of his own volition, the audience will check out. Why? Because that's not how life works. There needs to be a reason. Our character has to run into a high school sweetheart who is now a yoga instructor, or he needs to lose a bet, forcing him to run a marathon. Characters only take action after they are challenged by an outside force.

This principle is true in story because it's true in life. Human beings take action when their story challenges them to do so.

You would be surprised how many companies don't create obvious calls to action for their customers. A call to action involves communicating a clear and direct step our customer can take to overcome their challenge and return to a peaceful life. Without clear calls to action, people will not engage our brand.

In the fifth part of the StoryBrand Framework, I'll show you two calls to action that have worked for thousands of our clients. One call to action is direct, asking the customer for a purchase or to schedule an appointment. The other is a transitional call to action, furthering our relationship with the customer. Once we begin using both kinds of calls to action in our messaging, customers will understand exactly what we want them to do and decide whether to let us play a role in their story. Until we call our customers to action, they simply watch us, but when we call them to action (the right way), they will engage.

6. That Helps Them Avoid Failure

 STORYBRAND PRINCIPLE SIX: EVERY HUMAN BEING IS TRYING TO AVOID A TRAGIC ENDING.

Stories live and die on a single question: What's at stake? If nothing can be gained or lost, nobody cares. Will the hero disarm the bomb, or will people be killed? Will the guy get the girl, or will he be lonely and filled with self-doubt? These are the kinds of questions in the minds of a story-hungry audience.

If there is nothing at stake in a story, there is no story. Likewise, if there's nothing at stake in whether or not I buy your product, I'm not going to buy your product. After all, why should I?

Simply put, we must show people the cost of *not* doing business with us.

In the eighties, the fast-food chain Wendy's effectively asked America, "Where's the beef?" The implication was that their competitors weren't using enough meat. So what's at stake for choosing another brand over Wendy's? We might get stuck with a wimpy sandwich. Likewise, Whole Foods has built an enormous industry helping customers avoid the consequences of overly processed foods, and more recently Trader Joe's has come along to help customers avoid the consequences of Whole Foods' prices.

Brands that help customers avoid some kind of negativity in life (and let their customers know what that negativity is) engage customers for the same reason good stories captivate an audience: they define what's at stake.

In the sixth part of the StoryBrand Framework, I'll help you identify what's at stake in your customers' story as it relates to your brand. Before we move on, though, it's important to note that not all of the seven elements should be used evenly in your communication. Think of the StoryBrand Framework as a recipe for a loaf of bread. Failure is like salt: use too much and you'll ruin the flavor; leave it out and the recipe will taste bland. Regardless, the point is this: your story needs stakes.

7. And Ends in a Success

STORYBRAND PRINCIPLE SEVEN: NEVER ASSUME PEOPLE UNDERSTAND HOW YOUR BRAND CAN CHANGE THEIR LIVES. TELL THEM.

We must tell our customers how great their life can look if they buy our products and services. Ronald Reagan painted a picture of "a shining city on a hill."[2] Bill Clinton offered to help us "build a bridge to the twenty-first century."[3] During the dark and dreary Depression, Franklin Roosevelt used the song "Happy Days Are Here Again" as his official campaign song.[4] Likewise, Apple provides tools that allow us to express ourselves and be heard, Weight Watchers helps us lose weight and feel great, and Men's Wearhouse guarantees we will like the way we look.

Everybody wants to be taken somewhere. If we don't tell people where we're taking them, they'll engage another brand.

In the seventh part of the StoryBrand Framework, I'll elaborate on what is perhaps the most important element of your messaging strategy: offering a vision for how great a customer's life could be if they engage your products or services.

WHEN YOU FEEL CONFUSED, CLARIFY YOUR MESSAGE

Right about now your head may be spinning. Even though there are only seven parts to the framework, how do we narrow down our message so our marketing material starts working again?

We've created a tool to simplify the process. This tool is going to reduce the hassle of creating a clear message, save you time, entertain you as you use it, and motivate you to create marketing material that works. As I mentioned earlier, this tool is called the StoryBrand BrandScript, and it's going to become your new best friend.

You can create your StoryBrand BrandScript for free at mystorybrand.com, and it looks like this:

In the next seven chapters, I'm going to walk you through these seven elements and help you create your BrandScript. Once you're done, you'll no longer feel confused about how to talk about your products and services, and you'll have messages that powerfully engage potential customers.

The first project I'd like you to BrandScript is the one that represents your overall brand. Next you'll want to create a BrandScript for each division of your company, and after that, each product within each division. If you like, you can even create a BrandScript for each segment of your customer base. The uses of a StoryBrand BrandScript are endless.

Again, to create a BrandScript you can save, edit, and come back to over and over, go to mystorybrand.com. Because you bought this book, you get free access. Your StoryBrand BrandScript will be a powerful resource helping you organize and simplify your message, and you'll use it again and again. With the StoryBrand BrandScript tool, you will be able to see your brand narrative on a single page, which, again, will translate into a clear message you can use to grow your business.

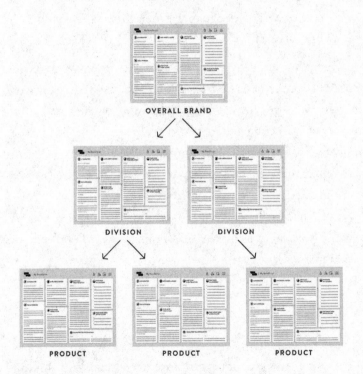

OVERALL BRAND

DIVISION   DIVISION

PRODUCT   PRODUCT   PRODUCT

CLARIFY YOUR MESSAGE SO CUSTOMERS LISTEN

As you walk through the seven parts of the StoryBrand Framework, simply follow these three steps:

1. Read each of the next seven chapters.
2. After you read each chapter, brainstorm potential messages you might use to populate your BrandScript.
3. Carefully look at your brainstorm and then decide on a specific message to use in each section of your BrandScript.

Once you complete your BrandScript at mystorybrand.com, you will have the basic messages to employ the SB7 Framework on your websites, in keynotes, in elevator pitches, and in all manner of marketing and messaging collateral. This means your messages will be simple, relevant, and repeatable. And remember: simple, clear messages that are relevant to your customers result in sales.

Every human being is already speaking the language of story, so when you begin using the SB7 Framework, you'll finally be speaking their language.

THE STAKES ARE HIGH

You're going to be tempted to move ahead and skip thinking deliberately about each of the seven parts of the framework. You've already got the BrandScript, after all, so why not just fill it out?

Amateur screenwriters make the same mistake. They think they know how a story works, so they start typing and a couple of months later can't figure out why their story is boring and unrelatable. I'll tell you why. They had an overview of the process but never bothered to learn the actual rules.

Each module of the SB7 Framework has set-in-stone rules you cannot break—or else customers won't find themselves in the story you're telling and will be much less likely to engage your brand.

Thousands of companies shut their doors every year, not because they don't have a great product, but because potential customers can't figure out how that product will make their lives better. If we don't closely analyze each element of our customers' story, they'll sense we don't care and move on to a competing brand that took the time to do the work.

Some of you are probably thinking it's too late. I mean, if it's printed in a book, everybody else is probably doing it. But are they? How many people read the first twenty pages of a book and then stop reading? I'd say most, which means you're already passing them. What would happen if you committed to executing this process and your competitor didn't? You'd win, wouldn't you? And how many people are actually going to put in the work even if they do read the book? Believe me, human nature tends toward complacency. Finish this process. Beat the competition. Clarify your message. Grow your company. The competition may be more talented than you are, but they will never outwork you if you don't let them. That's the one thing you get to control.

In the next seven chapters, I'll show you how to create a clear and compelling message that will organize your thoughts, simplify your marketing, and grow your company.

BUILDING YOUR STORYBRAND

When you're confused, create a StoryBrand BrandScript.

--- CHAPTER 4 ---

A CHARACTER

StoryBrand Principle One: The customer
is the hero, not your brand.

A story doesn't really pick up until the hero needs to disarm a bomb, win someone's heart, defeat a villain, or fight for their emotional or physical survival. A story starts with a hero who wants something. And then the question becomes: Will the hero get what she wants?

Before knowing what the hero wants, the audience has little interest in her fate. This is why screenwriters have to define the character's ambition within the first nine or so minutes of a film getting started. Will the underdog get the promotion? Will the runner finish the marathon? Will the team win the championship? These are the questions that keep an audience engaged for two hours.

As a brand it's important to define something your customer wants, because as soon as we define something our customer wants, we posit a story question in the mind of the customer: *Can this brand really help me get what I want?*

Recently a high-end resort hired us to help them clarify their message. Like many companies, they were experiencing an identity crisis. Their marketing collateral featured images of their restaurant, front desk, and staff. It all looked nice, but unless they were trying to sell their buildings, they weren't exactly inviting customers into a story.

What their customers wanted most, actually, was a luxurious, restful experience. After StoryBranding their resort, they changed the text on their website from long stories about themselves (which positioned them as the hero) to images of a warm bath, plush towels and robes, someone getting a massage in the spa, and a looping clip of a back-porch rocking chair against the backdrop of trees blowing in the wind along a golf course.

They replaced the text on their main page with short and powerful copy: "Find the luxury and rest you've been looking for." That became the mantra for the entire staff. This phrase was posted on their office walls, and to this day you can stop any team member from the sous chef to the groundskeeper and they will tell you their customers are looking for two things: luxury and rest. Defining exactly what their customer wanted brought clarity and camaraderie to the staff. Each member of the staff then understood his or her role in the story they were inviting their customers to engage in.

One university we worked with defined their customer's desire as "a hassle-free MBA you can complete after work." A landscaping company humorously defined their customer's ambition as "a yard that looks better than your neighbor's." A caterer we worked with in Los Angeles defined his customer's desire as "a mobile fine-dining experience in the environment of your choice."

When we identify something our customer wants and communicate it simply, the story we are inviting them into is given definition and direction.

Here are some more examples from companies we've worked with:

Financial Advisor: "A Plan for Your Retirement"
College Alumni Association: "Leave a Meaningful Legacy"
Fine-Dining Restaurant: "A Meal Everybody Will Remember"
Real Estate Agent: "The Home You've Dreamed About"
Bookstore: "A Story to Get Lost In"
Breakfast Bars: "A Healthy Start to Your Day"

When you define something your customer wants, the customer is invited to alter their story in your direction. If they see your brand as a trustworthy and reliable guide, they will likely engage.

OPEN A STORY GAP

In story terms, identifying a potential desire for your customer opens what's sometimes called a story gap. The idea is that you place a gap between a character and what they want. Moviegoers pay attention when there's a story gap because they wonder if and how that gap is going to be closed.

Jason Bourne is a spy who has amnesia, and we wonder if he'll find anyone to help him. When he meets a young woman named Marie, that gap closes, only for another to open. Bourne and

Marie have to flee the country. When they escape, that gap closes for yet another one to open. The cycle goes on and on, maintaining a taut grip on the audience's attention up until the finale.

To understand the power of a story gap is to understand what compels a human brain toward a desire. Even classical music follows this formula. Many classical sonatas can be broken into three sections: exposition, development, and recapitulation. The final section, recapitulation, is simply an altered version of the exposition that brings a sense of resolve. If that doesn't make sense, try singing "Twinkle, Twinkle, Little Star" without singing the final note on the word *are*. It will bother you to no end.

We also see this at work in poetry. When our ears hear Lord Byron's first line "She walks in beauty, like the night," a story gap has been opened. We are waiting to hear a word that rhymes with *night* and closes the open gap in our minds. Once we hear "Of cloudless climes and starry skies," our minds find a bit of resolution. Until the next line, that is.

The opening and closing of a story gap is a magnetic force that drives much of human behavior. Arousal is the opening of a story gap and sexual fulfillment brings its closing. Hunger is the opening of a story gap and a meal ushers its closing. There is little action in life that can't be explained by the opening and closing of various story gaps.

When we fail to define something our customer wants, we fail to open a story gap. When we don't open a story gap in our customers' mind, they have no motivation to engage us, because there is no question that demands resolution. Defining something our customer wants and featuring it in our marketing materials will open a story gap.

PARE DOWN THE CUSTOMER'S
AMBITION TO A SINGLE FOCUS

A critical mistake many organizations make in defining something their customers want is they don't pare down that desire to a single focus. I've had countless conversations with frustrated business leaders who push back at this point and say, "Wait, we provide about twenty-seven things our customers want. Can't we mention all of them?"

The answer is no, at least not yet. Until we've defined a specific desire and become known for helping people achieve it, we shouldn't add too many conflicting story gaps to our StoryBrand BrandScript.

This can be frustrating if your products and services fulfill many desires. The reality of a diverse brand, though, brings the same challenge many amateur screenwriters succumb to: they clutter the story by diluting their hero's desire with too many ambitions.

As you create a BrandScript for your overall brand, focus on one simple desire and then, as you create campaigns for each division and maybe even each product, you can identify more things your customer wants in the subplots of your overall brand.

On the following page you'll find a grid of what a diverse brand might look like using the tool of various StoryBrand BrandScripts.

At the highest level, the most important challenge for business leaders is to define something simple and relevant their customers want and to become known for delivering on that promise. Everything else is a subplot that, after having delivered on the customer's basic desire, will only serve to delight and surprise them all the more.

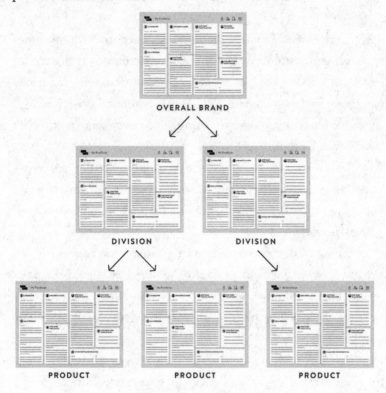

OVERALL BRAND

DIVISION   **DIVISION**

PRODUCT   **PRODUCT**   **PRODUCT**

CHOOSE A DESIRE RELEVANT TO THEIR SURVIVAL

Once a brand defines what their customer wants, they are often guilty of making the second mistake—what they've defined isn't related to the customer's sense of survival. In their desire to cast a wide net, they define a blob of a desire that is so vague, potential customers can't figure out why they need it in the first place.

A leadership expert recently asked for feedback on his brand.

As I reviewed his marketing material, I noticed he was making a critical mistake: in defining what his customer wanted, he was vague.

The idea behind his brand is that he imparts knowledge to potential leaders. He saw himself as a storehouse of leadership resources and wanted to be the go-to guy for achieving excellence. In fact, his tagline was "Inhale knowledge, exhale success."

Seems clear enough, but is it? What does exhaling success even mean? He was making potential customers burn too many mental calories to figure out how he was going to help them survive and thrive.

I recommended he make an edit to his message. Instead of saying, "Inhale knowledge, exhale success," simply say, "Helping you become everyone's favorite leader."

Becoming everyone's favorite leader means the customer would be more respected and better connected to a tribe, they'd have greater social and career opportunities, and much more. Exhaling success sounded nice, but thriving as the leader of a tribe is directly connected to survival. People will always choose a story that helps them survive and thrive.

Fortunately, he liked the idea, mostly because that's what he was already doing. Defining something the customer wants and connecting it with the customer's desire for survival opened an enticing story gap.

What Does Survival Mean?

When I say *survival*, I'm talking about that primitive desire we all have to be safe, healthy, happy, and strong. Survival simply means we have the economic and social resources to eat, drink, reproduce, and fend off foes.

So what kinds of desires fit under this definition? Well, too many to count, but consider these examples:

> *Conserving financial resources.* In order to survive and thrive, your customers may need to conserve resources. In simple terms, this means they may need to save money. If your brand can help them save money, you've tapped into a survival mechanism. Walmart has built their brand on the promise of everyday low prices. Their tagline "Save Money. Live Better" further communicates savings and value and thus taps into a basic function of survival, the conservation of resources.
>
> *Conserving time.* In developed countries, most of our customers have thankfully moved beyond the hunter-gatherer stage of survival. They are familiar, then, with the notion of opportunity costs. Can your housecleaning service give your customers more time to work on other things or more time to spend with family? Then they might be interested.
>
> *Building social networks.* If our brand can help us find community, we've tapped into yet another survival mechanism. We only think we're being nice when we bring our coworkers coffee, but what if we're actually being nice because our primitive brains want to make sure we are connected to a tribe in case the bad guys come knocking at the door? Add this to the fact that human beings have a strong desire to nurture and be nurtured, and we've tapped into yet another survival mechanism.
>
> *Gaining status.* Luxury brands like Mercedes and Rolex don't make much practical sense in terms of survival, right? In fact, spending lots of money buying a luxury car

when a more common brand would do the trick seems counter to our survival, doesn't it? Not when you consider the importance of status. Status, in any tribe, is a survival mechanism. It projects a sense of abundance that may attract powerful allies, repel potential foes (like a lion with a loud roar), and if we're into shallow companions, might even help us secure a mate. Rolex, Mercedes, Louis Vuitton, and other luxury brands are truly selling more than just cars and watches; they're selling an identity associated with power, prestige, and refinement.

Accumulating resources. If the products and services you offer help people make money or accumulate much-needed resources, that will quickly translate into a person's desire for survival. With more money, our customers will have more opportunity to secure many of the other survival resources they may need. Many StoryBrand clients run business-to-business offerings (StoryBrand itself is a business-to-business company), so offering increased productivity, increased revenue, or decreased waste are powerful associations with the need for a business (or an individual) to survive and thrive.

The innate desire to be generous. None of the desires I've listed are evil. They can all be taken too far, but the reality is we are designed to survive. Still, we should be comforted by the fact that nearly all human beings have an enormous potential for generosity. Achieving an aspirational identity of being sacrificial actually helps us survive (fends off foes, decreases outside criticism, helps earn trust in our tribe, and so on), but it also taps into something truly redemptive: we want other people to survive too.

Most people are not nearly as Darwinian in their thinking as we've been led to believe. We are empathetic and caring creatures who will gladly sacrifice for the well-being of others, often in anonymity. The truth is we aren't only interested in our own survival; we're interested in the survival of others. Especially those who have not been given the opportunities we enjoy.

The desire for meaning. Viktor Frankl was right when he contended with Sigmund Freud, insinuating that the chief desire of man is not pleasure but meaning. In fact, in his book *Man's Search for Meaning*, Frankl argued convincingly that man was actually most tempted to distract himself with pleasure when his life was void of meaning.[1] So how do we offer potential customers a sense of meaning? Not unlike giving our customers the opportunity to be generous, we invite them to participate in something greater than themselves. A movement. A cause to champion. A valiant fight against a real villain, be that villain flesh and blood or a harmful philosophy.

WHAT'S THE STORY QUESTION FOR YOUR CUSTOMER?

When I offered my executive coach friend the tagline "Helping you become the leader everybody loves," his customers' brains were able to translate that message into multiple survival categories, including social networks, status, the innate desire to be generous, the opportunity to gain resources, and even the desire for deeper meaning.

In business, if we don't communicate clearly, we shrink. When we're motivating a team, convincing shareholders, or engaging customers, we must define a desire our customers have or we will have failed to open a story gap and our audience will ignore us. Remember, customers want to know where you can take them. Unless you identify something they want, it's doubtful they will listen.

Imagine your customer is a hitchhiker. You pull over to give him a ride, and the one burning question on his mind is simply *Where are you going?* But as he approaches, you roll down the window and start talking about your mission statement, or how your grandfather built this car with his bare hands, or how your road-trip playlist is all 1980s alternative. This person doesn't care. All he wants to do is get to San Francisco with a flower in his hair!

The goal for our branding should be that every potential customer knows exactly where we want to take them: a luxury resort where they can get some rest, to become the leader everybody loves, or to save money and live better.

If you randomly asked a potential customer where your brand wants to take them, would they be able to answer? Would they be able to repeat back to you exactly what your brand offers? If not, your brand is suffering the cost of confusion. You can fix this. Define a desire for your customer, and the story you're inviting customers into will have a powerful hook.

CLARIFY YOUR MESSAGE SO CUSTOMERS LISTEN

- Go to mystorybrand.com and either create a StoryBrand BrandScript or log in to your existing BrandScript.
- Either alone or with a team, brainstorm what potential desires your customers might have that you can fulfill.
- Make a decision. Choose something your customer wants and fill in the "character" module of your StoryBrand BrandScript.
- Read the next chapter and repeat this process for the next section of your BrandScript.

A CHARACTER

WHAT DO THEY WANT?

Once you fill out the first module of your StoryBrand BrandScript, you'll be on your way to inviting customers into an incredible story. At this point, they're interested in you and what you offer. But what can we do to entice them even further into a story? Let's move on to part 2 and find out!

You will be tempted to fill out the rest of your StoryBrand BrandScript, but I encourage you to read the chapter associated with each module to be sure you're filling it out correctly. Once you've completed your first BrandScript, section 3 of this book will help you create simple, effective marketing tools.

CHAPTER 5

HAS A PROBLEM

StoryBrand Principle Two: Companies tend to sell solutions to external problems, but customers buy solutions to internal problems.

Now that you've entered into your customers' story, how do you increase their interest in your brand? You borrow another play from the storyteller's playbook; you start talking about the problems your customers face.

Identifying our customers' problems deepens their interest in the story we are telling. Every story is about somebody who is trying to solve a problem, so when we identify our customers' problems, they recognize us as a brand that understands them.

The problem is the "hook" of a story, and if we don't identify our customers' problems, the story we are telling will fall flat. As soon as the conflict in a story is resolved, audiences stop paying attention. As the novelist James Scott Bell says, "Readers want to fret."[1] It's true in story and it's true in branding.

If Jason Bourne were to get a call thirty minutes into the first *Bourne Identity* movie and a gentle, calming voice began to explain who Jason really was, why he'd suffered amnesia, and that the government was offering him a pension along with a house on the coast, then no one would keep watching. The reason to pay attention would be gone.

It bears repeating. The more we talk about the problems our customers experience, the more interest they will have in our brand.

HOW TO TALK ABOUT YOUR CUSTOMERS' PROBLEMS

In the second module of the StoryBrand Framework, we're going to look at three elements of conflict that will increase customer interest, ratchet up engagement, and give a greater depth of meaning to the story our brand is telling.

First, though, let's start with the root of where all this conflict is coming from. I'm talking about one of the most dynamic, interesting characters in any story: the villain.

Every Story Needs a Villain

The villain is the number one device storytellers use to give conflict a clear point of focus.

Screenwriters and novelists know the stronger, more evil, more dastardly the villain, the more sympathy we will have for the hero and the more the audience will want them to win in the end. This translates into audience engagement.

How sympathetic would Batman be without the Joker?

Luke Skywalker without Darth Vader? Harry Potter without Voldemort? Superman without Kryptonite? (Let's be honest, Lex Luthor isn't that interesting of a bad guy.)

If we want our customers' ears to perk up when we talk about our products and services, we should position those products and services as weapons they can use to defeat a villain. And the villain should be dastardly.

The villain doesn't have to be a person, but without question it should have personified characteristics. If we're selling time-management software, for instance, we might vilify the idea of *distractions.* Could we offer our product as a weapon customers could use to stop distractions in their tracks? Sounds kind of dramatic, right? And yet distractions are what's deluding our customers' potential, wrecking their families, stealing their sanity, and costing them enormous amounts of time and money. Distractions, then, make for great little villains.

Now that I've pointed out the technique of vilifying our customers' challenges, you'll see it in television commercials all the time. Who knew that those dust bunnies collecting along the baseboards of our houses move around in animated, criminal gangs wearing leather jackets, coordinating their devilish efforts to ruin our floors? Ah, that is until they meet their match: the new mop from ACME Mop Company.

Advertisers personify the problems their customers face in order to capture their imagination and give their frustrations a focal point. Fuzzy hairballs with squeaky voices living in your drains, making nests, and clogging up the pipes? Yellow globs of living, breathing, talking plaque vacationing between your teeth? These are all personified versions of conflict. They're all villains.

Here are four characteristics that make for a good villain on your StoryBrand BrandScript:

1. **The villain should be a root source.** Frustration, for example, is not a villain; frustration is what a villain makes us feel. High taxes, rather, are a good example of a villain.
2. **The villain should be relatable.** When people hear us talk about the villain, they should immediately recognize it as something they disdain.
3. **The villain should be singular.** One villain is enough. A story with too many villains falls apart for lack of clarity.
4. **The villain should be real.** Never go down the path of being a fearmonger. There are plenty of actual villains out there to fight. Let's go after them on behalf of our customers.

Is there a villain in your customers' story? Of course there is. What is the chief source of conflict that your products and services defeat? Talk about this villain. The more you talk about the villain, the more people will want a tool to help them defeat the villain.

Later, when you're creating your BrandScript, I'll ask you to brainstorm what kind of villain your customer faces. For now, though, let's look closely at the kinds of conflict this villain causes. Once we understand our customers' problems, we'll have a better idea how to talk to them in such a way that they engage.

The Three Levels of Conflict

A villain is the antagonist because the villain causes the hero serious problems. That's obvious. But what's less obvious is that in a story, there are three levels of problems that work together to capture a reader's or a moviegoer's imagination.

The three levels of problems heroes (and customers) face are

External Problems
Internal Problems
Philosophical Problems

In a story, a villain initiates an external problem that causes the character to experience an internal frustration that is, quite simply, philosophically wrong. These are also the three levels of problems a customer hopes to solve when they buy a product.

I know that sounds complicated, but let's take a closer look at each level of conflict so we know exactly which of our customers' frustrations to talk about as we clarify our message.

EXTERNAL PROBLEMS

In literature, a villain's job is to wreak havoc on the hero, to place barriers between them and their desperate desire for stability. But ill intentions aren't enough. Something, that is, some *thing* (or things) must represent this barrier. Enter the "external problem."

In stories, the external problem is often a physical, tangible problem the hero must overcome in order to save the day. The problem might manifest itself as a ticking time bomb or a runaway bus, or maybe even a combination of the two: a bomb on a bus that will go off if Keanu Reeves doesn't keep the speed above fifty miles per hour!

The external problem works like a prized chess piece set between the hero and the villain, and each is trying to control the piece so they can win the game.

For Billy Beane in the movie *Moneyball*, the external problem is the need to win baseball games. For Matthew Broderick in the movie *WarGames*, it's a piece of rogue software that has taken over the American government's computer system and attempts to wage war against the Soviets.

But what does the existence of an external problem in a story have to do with branding? Well, most of us are in the business of solving external problems. We provide insurance or clothes or soccer balls. If we own a restaurant, the external problem we solve is hunger. The external problem a plumber fixes might be a leaky pipe, just like a pest-control guy might solve the external problem of termites in the attic.

Brainstorming what external problems you solve will be the easiest part of creating your StoryBrand BrandScript. It's usually pretty obvious. But you'd be wrong to think the reason people call you, walk through your door, or visit your website is limited to the resolution of an external problem. Something else is going on.

INTERNAL PROBLEMS

By limiting our marketing messages to only external problems, we neglect a principle that is costing us thousands and potentially millions of dollars. That principle is this: *Companies tend to sell solutions to external problems, but people buy solutions to internal problems.*

The purpose of an external problem in a story is to manifest an internal problem. If I wrote a movie about a guy who simply needed to disarm a bomb, audiences would lose interest. What storytellers and screenwriters do, then, is create a backstory of frustration in the hero's life.

In the movie *Moneyball*, for instance, Billy Beane failed in his playing career and so was filled with self-doubt about whether he could redeem himself as a general manager. In *Star Wars*, Luke Skywalker was told by his uncle that he was too young to join the resistance, so he doubted his ability until the very end.

In almost every story the hero struggles with the same question: *Do I have what it takes?* This question can make them feel frustrated, incompetent, and confused. The sense of self-doubt is what makes a movie about baseball relatable to a soccer mom and a romantic comedy relatable to a truck-driving husband.

What stories teach us is that people's internal desire to resolve a frustration is a greater motivator than their desire to solve an external problem.

This is where most brands make a critical mistake. By assuming our customers only want to resolve external problems, we fail to engage the deeper story they're actually living. The truth is, the external problems we solve are causing frustrations in their lives and, just like in a story, it's those frustrations that are motivating them to call you.

After their near collapse, Apple didn't find their footing until Steve Jobs understood that people felt intimidated (internal problem) by computers and wanted a simpler interface with technology. In one of the most powerful advertising campaigns in history, Apple showed a simple, hip, fun character who just wanted to take photos and listen to music and write books next to a not-so-hip tech nerd who wanted to talk about the inner workings of his operating system. The campaign positioned Apple Computers as the company to go to if you wanted to enjoy life and express yourself but felt intimidated by all the tech talk. What was the internal problem Apple identified? It was the sense of intimidation most people felt about computers. Apple started selling more than computers; they started selling a resolution to the problem of customer intimidation. Understanding their customers' internal problem is one of the reasons Apple achieved such growth and created passionate brand evangelists.

The only reason our customers buy from us is because the external problem we solve is frustrating them in some way. If we can identify that frustration, put it into words, and offer to resolve it along with the original external problem, something special happens. We bond with our customers because we've positioned ourselves more deeply into their narrative.

For example, if we own a house-painting business, our customer's external problem might be an unsightly home. The internal problem, however, may involve a sense of embarrassment about having the ugliest home on the street. Knowing this, our marketing could offer "Paint That Will Make Your Neighbors Jealous."

What Frustrations Do Our Products Resolve?

Recently, the rental-car company National got my business by understanding my internal frustration. I used to rent from a company that got on my nerves. Normally when I get off a plane I don't feel like making small talk. The staff at the company I used to rent cars from had a policy of chitchatting with their customers. They even used a script. First they asked whether I was in town for business or pleasure, then they asked about the weather where I came from. On and on it went. I heard this script so many times I started having fun beating them to their own talking points. I'd often jump ahead on their script and ask the clerk, "Are you going to be able to have a little downtime while you're in town?" They'd just stare blankly at me because I'd hijacked their line.

One day, though, I was watching television and a commercial came on for National. It showed a guy walking through the rental office without talking to anybody. The character talked about how he hated having to make conversation with salespeople and how he loved walking straight to his car. I immediately changed rental car companies and have been happy ever since.

Speaking of car companies, CarMax is a chain of used car dealerships that aims most of their marketing collateral at the internal problem a customer experiences when looking for a used car, namely having to interact with a used-car salesman.

If you've ever walked onto a used-car lot, you know the feeling. It's as though you're about to tangle with a professional wrestler.

Knowing their customers don't want to haggle over prices or risk buying a lemon, CarMax's business strategy is aimed at you not having to feel lied to, cheated, or worked over in your car-buying experience. To do this, they have an agreement plan with their customers that ensures the price on the car is the price you'll pay and lets you know their salespeople aren't compensated on commission. They also highlight their quality certification and inspection process that ensures every car they sell is reliable.[2]

The external problem CarMax resolves is the need for a car, of course, but they hardly advertise about cars at all. They focus on their customers' internal problems and, in doing so, entered one of the least-trusted industries in America and created a $15 billion franchise.[3]

Likewise, Starbucks exploded by not just offering customers a cup of coffee but by giving them a comfortable, sophisticated environment in which to relax. Customers felt good about them-selves when they walked into a Starbucks. Starbucks was deliv-ering more value than just coffee; they were delivering a sense of sophistication and enthusiasm about life. They were also offer-ing a place for people to meet in which they could experience affiliation and belonging. Starbucks changed American culture from hanging out in diners and bars to hanging out in a local, Italian-style coffee shop.

In understanding how their customers wanted to feel, Starbucks took a product that Americans were used to paying fifty cents for (or drinking for almost free at home or at work) and were able to charge three or four dollars per cup. Starbucks customers are willing to pay more for their coffee because they sense greater value with each cup.

Framing our products as a resolution to both external and internal problems increases the perceived value (and I would argue, actual value) of those products.

Later, I'll guide you through a brainstorming exercise help-ing you identify some of your customers' internal problems, but before that, let's look at a third kind of problem our custom-ers experience. This third level of problem can take a story over the top, have audiences standing on their seats, and is one of the main reasons a film will win Best Picture at the Academy Awards. And it has the same kind of power when it comes to helping us turn disinterested customers into brand fanatics.

PHILOSOPHICAL PROBLEMS

The philosophical problem in a story is about something even larger than the story itself. It's about the question *why*. Why does this story matter in the overall epic of humanity?

Why is it important that Tommy Boy save his dad's company? I'll tell you why, because the people trying to take Tommy Boy down are lying thieves. This is a comedic story about honesty, family, integrity, and hard work versus deception, greed, and trickery.

Why is it important that Hamlet avenge his father's death? Because his uncle is getting away with murder.

Why is it important that Bridget Jones find love? Because the beauty and worth of every person deserves to be recognized and cherished by another.

A philosophical problem can best be talked about using terms like *ought* and *shouldn't*. "Bad people shouldn't be allowed to win" or "People ought to be treated fairly."

In the movie *The King's Speech*, the external problem is King George's stutter. This external problem manifests the internal frustration and self-doubt the king struggles with. He simply doesn't believe he has what it takes to lead his country. Philosophically, though, the stakes are much greater. Because the king must unify his people against the Nazis, the story takes on the philosophical problem of good versus evil.

In *Jerry Maguire*, the philosophical question revolves around whether people are worth more than the money they can bring in. *Romeo and Juliet* asks whether romantic love is more important than family squabbles and tribal unrest.

What's the Deeper Meaning?

People want to be involved in a story that is larger than themselves. Brands that give customers a voice in a larger narrative add value to their products by giving their customers a deeper sense of meaning.

After creating their BrandScript, a global consulting firm we worked with began to talk about how everybody deserved to work for a great manager. A pet-store owner who came to us hung a sign in her window that said, "Pets deserve to eat healthy food too." A fun-loving travel agent came to us and adopted the seasonal line "Because this summer should be remembered forever."

Before music went digital, Tower Records promoted their chain of record stores using the tagline "No music, no life." Not only did the tagline help them sell more than a billion dollars in records each year, but they sold thousands of bumper stickers and T-shirts featuring the tagline to fans who wanted to associate with the philosophical belief that music mattered.

Is there a deeper story your brand contributes to? Can your products be positioned as tools your customers can use to fight back against something that ought not be? If so, let's include some philosophical stakes in our messaging.

The Perfect Brand Promise

If we really want to satisfy our customers, we can offer much more than products or services; we can offer to resolve an external, internal, and philosophical problem whenever they engage our business.

Storytellers use this formula to endear audiences all the time. When Luke shoots the photon torpedo through the little hole in the Death Star, he actually resolves the external problem of destroying the Death Star, the internal problem that had him wondering whether he had what it took to be a Jedi, and the philosophical problem of good versus evil, all with the press of a button.

When these three levels of problems are resolved in one shot, the audience experiences a sense of pleasure and relief, causing them to love the story. This scene is often called the "climactic" or "obligatory" scene, and it is arguably the most important scene in the movie because every other scene builds toward it in some way.

The resolution of the hero's external, internal, and philosophical problem is the reason we cried when Woody and Buzz were reunited with Andy in *Toy Story*, and it's why we felt so deeply when Private Ryan was rescued by Captain John Miller.

This formula works because human beings experience three levels of problems in their everyday lives. They aren't just looking for a resolution to one level of problem; they're hoping for a resolution to all three.

If we really want our business to grow, we should position our products as the resolution to an external, internal, and philosophical problem and frame the "Buy Now" button as the action a customer must take to create closure in their story.

Let's look at how some successful brands we all know about have positioned the purchasing of their products as the resolution to external, internal, and philosophical problems:

TESLA MOTOR CARS:
> **Villain:** Gas guzzling, inferior technology
> **External:** I need a car.
> **Internal:** I want to be an early adopter of new technology.
> **Philosophical:** My choice of car ought to help save the environment.

NESPRESSO HOME COFFEE MACHINES:
> **Villain:** Coffee machines that make bad coffee
> **External:** I want better-tasting coffee at home.

Internal: I want my home coffee machine to make me feel sophisticated.

Philosophical: I shouldn't have to be a barista to make a gourmet coffee at home.

EDWARD JONES FINANCIAL PLANNING:

Villain: Financial firms that don't listen to their customers

External: I need investment help.

Internal: I'm confused about how to do this (especially with all the tech-driven resources out there).

Philosophical: If I'm going to invest my money, I deserve an advisor who will thoughtfully explain things in person.

WHAT CHALLENGES ARE YOU HELPING YOUR CUSTOMER OVERCOME?

The idea of identifying a villain that is causing an internal, external, and philosophical problem may seem daunting, but it will come to you if you commit to working it out in a brainstorming session. But be careful. A large problem most of our clients face is they want to include three villains and seven external problems and four internal problems, and so on. But, as I've already mentioned, stories are best when they are simple and clear. We are going to have to make choices.

Is there a single villain your brand stands against? And what external problem is that villain causing? How is that external problem making your customers feel? And why is it unjust for people to have to suffer at the hands of this villain?

These are the four questions we want to answer in the problem section of our StoryBrand BrandScript, and when we do, the story our brand is telling will take shape because our hero, the customer who wants something, is being challenged. Will they win? Will their problems be resolved?

Perhaps. The thing is, they will have to engage your brand to find out.

CLARIFY YOUR MESSAGE SO CUSTOMERS LISTEN

- Go to mystorybrand.com and either create a BrandScript or log in to your existing BrandScript.
- Either alone or with a team, brainstorm all of the literal and metaphorical villains your brand takes a stand against.
- Brainstorm the external problems your brand resolves. Is there one that seems to represent the widest swath of products?
- Brainstorm the internal problem (frustration or doubt) your customers are feeling as it relates to your brand. Is there one that stands out as a universal experience for your customers?
- Is your brand part of a larger, more important story? Is there a philosophical wrong your brand stands against?

HAS A PROBLEM

VILLAIN
_____
_____
_____

INTERNAL
_____
_____
_____

EXTERNAL
_____
_____
_____

PHILOSOPHICAL
_____
_____
_____

- Once you finish your brainstorming session, make the four StoryBrand BrandScript decisions that will allow you to fill out part 2.

CHAPTER 6

AND MEETS A GUIDE

StoryBrand Principle Three: Customers
aren't looking for another hero;
they're looking for a guide.

Shakespeare was right—a person's life is made up of many acts. As a book writer, though, I prefer to see these acts as chapters. If you look back on your life, you'll likely see them too. There is the chapter when you grew up poor and the chapter when you began to understand the importance of relationships. There is the chapter when you realized you were good at math or sports, and there was the chapter when you left home to start out on your own.

No two lives are the same, and yet we share common chapters. Every human being is on a transformational journey.

It's easy to recognize these chapters by their events, or what writer and story scholar James Scott Bell calls "doorways of no return."[1] This might have been our parents' divorce, our first crush, a rejection from somebody we loved, or having absolutely nailed the moonwalk when the crowd gathered around us at the junior high dance.

In stories, events mark the beginnings and endings of our chapters. But if we look closer, we will see something else or, more accurately, somebody else.

The events that define our chapters are often instigated or interpreted by mystical characters that help us along the way. In a story there are many names for these characters, but I choose to call them *guides*.

In his book *The Seven Basic Plots*, Christopher Booker describes the introduction of the guide into the story this way:

> A hero or heroine falls under a dark spell which eventually traps them in some wintry state, akin to a living death: physical or spiritual imprisonment, sleep, sickness or some other form of enchantment. For a long time they languish in this frozen condition. Then a miraculous act of redemption takes place, focused on a particular figure who helps to liberate the hero or heroine from imprisonment. From the depths of darkness they are brought up into glorious light.[2]

EVERY HERO IS LOOKING FOR A GUIDE

When I talk about a guide, I'm talking about our mother and father when they sat us down to talk about integrity, or a football coach who helped us understand the importance of working hard and believing we could accomplish more than we ever thought possible. Guides might include the authors of poems we've read, leaders who moved the world into new territory, therapists who helped us make sense of our problems, and yes, even brands that offered us encouragement and tools to help us overcome a challenge.

If a hero solves her own problem in a story, the audience will tune out. Why? Because we intuitively know if she could solve her own problem, she wouldn't have gotten into trouble in the first place. Storytellers use the guide character to encourage the hero and equip them to win the day.

You've seen the guide in nearly every story you've read, listened to, or watched: Frodo has Gandalf, Katniss has Haymitch, and Luke Skywalker has Yoda. Hamlet was "guided" by his father's ghost, and Romeo was taught the ways of love by Juliet.

Just like in stories, human beings wake up every morning self-identifying as a hero. They are troubled by internal, external, and philosophical conflicts, and they know they can't solve these problems on their own.

The fatal mistake some brands make, especially young brands who believe they need to prove themselves, is they position themselves as the hero in the story instead of the guide. As I've already mentioned, a brand that positions itself as the hero is destined to lose.

The Fatal Mistake

The fatal ramifications of positioning our brand as the hero could be huge. Consider the failure of the music streaming service Tidal. Never heard of it? There's a good reason. Rapper Jay Z founded the company with a personal investment of a whopping $56 million with a mission to "get everyone to respect music again."[3] Instead of being owned by music studios or tech companies, Tidal would be owned by musicians, allowing them to cut out the middleman and take their products directly to the market. As a result, the artists would pocket more of the profits.

Sounds like a great plan. But Jay Z failed to consider the mistake of positioning himself and other artists as the heroes. Were artists going to buy music from each other? No. He needed to position the customer, not the artist, as the hero.

In the months leading up to the launch of Tidal, Jay Z recruited sixteen well-known musicians who agreed to release exclusive content on his platform in exchange for a percentage of equity. In their multimillion-dollar rollout, the artists stood shoulder to shoulder at a press conference to explain their mission. Predictably, this is where everything fell apart.

If only Jay Z, in other ways a virtual genius, had understood the age-old rules of story, he might have avoided walking into a field of land mines.

"Water is free," Jay Z quipped. "Music is $6 but no one wants to pay for music." He continued, somewhat confusingly, "You should drink free water from the tap—it's a beautiful thing. And if you want to hear the most beautiful song, then support the artist."[4]

Social media, especially Twitter, eviscerated Jay Z and Tidal. Thousands reminded him to check with the people who paid his bills to discover water wasn't actually free. Overnight, an artist who built his career speaking for the people sounded entitled. The public became nauseated listening to a row of famous, multimillionaire musicians guilt-trip them into paying more for their music. The crucial mistake: Jay Z failed to answer the one question lingering in the subconscious of every hero customer: *How are you helping me win the day?* Tidal existed to help the artists win the day, not customers. And so it failed.

Always position your customer as the hero and your brand as the guide. Always. If you don't, you will die.

The Story Is Not About Us

The larger point here is simple: the day we stop losing sleep over the success of our business and start losing sleep over the success of our customers is the day our business will start growing again.

If we are tempted to position our brand as the hero because heroes are strong and capable and the center of attention, we should take a step back. In stories, the hero is never the strongest character. Heroes are often ill-equipped and filled with self-doubt. They don't know if they have what it takes. They are often reluctant, being thrown into the story rather than willingly engaging the plot. The guide, however, has already "been there and done that" and has conquered the hero's challenge in their own backstory.

The guide, not the hero, is the one with the most authority. Still, the story is rarely about the guide. The guide simply plays a role. The story must always be focused on the hero, and if a storyteller (or business leader) forgets this, the audience will get confused about who the story is really about and they will lose interest. This is true in business, in politics, and even in your own family. People are looking for a guide to help them, not another hero.

Those who realize the epic story of life is not about them but actually about the people around them somehow win in the end. It's counterintuitive, but it's true. In fact, leaders who think the story of life is all about them may achieve temporary successes but are usually remembered in history's narrative as a villain.

THE TWO CHARACTERISTICS OF A GUIDE

We have seen hundreds if not thousands of businesses experience an increase in customer engagement once they started positioning themselves as the guide. After filtering their message through the StoryBrand Framework, business leaders realize their websites, e-mail blasts, digital ads, television commercials, and even their elevator pitches have been facing the wrong direction. Simply turning our focus to the customer and offering them a heroic role in a meaningful story is enough to radically change the way we talk about, and even do, business. So what do we have to do to be recognized as the guide in our customers' lives?

The two things a brand must communicate to position themselves as the guide are

Empathy
Authority

When Luke Skywalker meets Yoda, he encounters the perfect guide. Yoda is the endearing character who understands Luke's dilemma and empathetically coaches him to use the Force. This empathy would go nowhere, of course, were it not for Yoda's authority as a Jedi himself. Yoda understands Luke's dilemma and has mastered the skills Luke must develop if he is going to win the day.

The guide must have this precise one-two punch of empathy and authority in order to move the hero and the story along. These are the characteristics the hero is looking for, and when she senses them, she knows she's found her guide.

Express Empathy

When Bill Clinton delivered his now-famous line "I feel your pain" in 1992, he did more than just clinch a victory over George H. W. Bush; he positioned himself as the guide in the American voters' story. A guide expresses an understanding of the pain and frustration of their hero. In fact, many pundits believe Clinton locked up the election during a town hall debate in which Bush gave a rambling answer to a young woman when she asked what the national debt meant to the average American. Clinton countered Bush's linear, cerebral answer by asking the woman if she knew anybody who'd lost their job. He asked whether it pained her that she had friends out of work, and when the woman said yes, he went on to explain how the national debt is tied to the well-being of every American, even her and her friends.[5] That's empathy.

When we empathize with our customers' dilemma, we create a bond of trust. People trust those who understand them, and they trust brands that understand them too.

Oprah Winfrey, an undeniably successful guide to millions, once explained the three things every human being wants most are to be seen, heard, and understood. This is the essence of empathy.

Empathetic statements start with words like, "We understand how it feels to . . ." or "Nobody should have to experience . . ." or "Like you, we are frustrated by . . ." or, in the case of one Toyota commercial inviting Toyota owners to engage their local Toyota service center, simply, "We care about your Toyota."

Expressing empathy isn't difficult. Once we've identified our customers' internal problems, we simply need to let them know we understand and would like to help them find a resolution. Scan your marketing material and make sure you've told your customers that you care. Customers won't know you care until you tell them.

ARE YOU LIKE ME?

Empathy is more than just sentimental slogans, though. Real empathy means letting customers know we see them as we see ourselves. Customers look for brands they have something in common with. Remember, the human brain likes to conserve calories, and so when a customer realizes they have a lot in common with a brand, they fill in all the unknown nuances with trust. Essentially, the customer batches their thinking, meaning they're thinking in "chunks" rather than details. Commonality, whether taste in music or shared values, is a powerful marketing tool.

A recent Discover Card television campaign tapped into the power of empathy by featuring people who call customer service and end up talking to an exact replica of themselves. The message? Discover Card will take care of you the same way you would take care of yourself.

Demonstrate Authority

Nobody likes a know-it-all and nobody wants to be preached at. Brands that lord their expertise over the masses turn people off. For this reason, many marketing experts say we shouldn't express authority at all, that what people want is a brand that puts their arm around their customer's shoulder and walks alongside them as an equal. But this isn't completely true.

Imagine walking into a nutritionist's office for the first time, determined to get into the best shape of your life.

"I'd like to lose thirty pounds," you tell her. "It's been a struggle for a long time, but I'm ready."

What would you do if the nutritionist looked back at you and said, "Me too!"

It wouldn't take you long to realize you'd chosen the wrong nutritionist.

When I talk about authority, I'm really talking about competence. When looking for a guide, a hero trusts somebody who knows what they're doing. The guide doesn't have to be perfect, but the guide needs to have serious experience helping other heroes win the day.

So how do we express our authority without bragging about ourselves so much that we step into the role of hero?

As customers view our websites, commercials, or e-mails, they simply want to check off a box in the back of their minds that gives them confidence in our ability to help them.

There are four easy ways to add just the right amount of authority to our marketing.

1. **Testimonials:** Let others do the talking for you. If you have satisfied customers, place a few testimonials on your website. Testimonials give potential customers the gift of going second. They know others have worked with you and attained success. Avoid stacking ten to twenty testimonials; otherwise you run the risk of positioning yourself as the hero. Three is a great number to start with and will serve the need most customers have to make sure you know what you are doing. Also, avoid rambling testimonials that heap endless praise on your brand. It won't take long for a customer to trust you, so keep a testimonial brief.

2. **Statistics:** How many satisfied customers have you helped? How much money have you helped them save? By what percentage have their businesses grown since they started working with you? A simple statement like the e-mail marketing platform Infusionsoft's "125,000 users trust [our] award-winning automation software"[6] is all your potential customer needs. Moreover, this scratches the itch of the left-brained consumer who loves numbers, statistics, and facts.

3. **Awards:** If you've won a few awards for your work, feel free to include small logos or indications of those awards at the bottom of your page. Again, there's no need to make a big deal about it, but awards go a long way in earning your customer's trust, even if they've never heard of the award.

4. **Logos:** If you provide a business-to-business product or service, place logos of known businesses you've worked with in your marketing collateral. Customers want to know you've helped other businesses overcome their same challenges. When they recognize another business you've worked with, it provides social proof you have the ability to help them win the day.

Take a minute to scan your marketing material and ask yourself whether you've demonstrated competency. Remember, you don't have to brag about yourself. Testimonials, logos, awards, and statistics will allow customers to check the "trust" box in the back of their minds. The questions they're asking themselves are, "Does this brand know what they're doing? Is investing my time and money going to be worth it? Can they really help me solve my problem?"

HOW TO MAKE A GREAT
FIRST IMPRESSION

When people meet your brand, it's as though they are meeting a person. They're wondering if the two of you will get along, whether you can help them live a better life, whether they want to associate their identity with your brand, and ultimately whether they can trust you.

Harvard Business professor Amy Cuddy has spent more than fifteen years studying how business leaders can make a positive first impression. Cuddy distilled her research into two questions people subconsciously ask when meeting someone new: "Can I trust this person?" and "Can I respect this person?" In her book *Presence*, Cuddy explains human beings value trust so highly, it's only after trust is established that a person begins to consider getting to know us further.[7]

When we express empathy, we help our customers answer Cuddy's first question, "Can I trust this person?"

Demonstrating competence helps our customers answer the second question, "Can I respect this person?"

The same two characteristics that help us make a great first impression with people at a cocktail party also work to help our brand make a great first impression with potential customers.

Once we express empathy and demonstrate authority, we can position our brand as the guide our customer has been looking for. This will make a significant difference in the way they remember us, understand us, and ultimately, engage with our products and services.

That said, even though our customers like us and trust us, it doesn't mean they're going to place an order. There is still a yawning chasm between a customer's affection and their decision to invest their hard-earned money in what we're offering. What are they looking for next? We'll talk about it in the next chapter.

For now, though, brainstorm how you can position yourself as the guide in your customer's life by expressing empathy and demonstrating authority.

CLARIFY YOUR MESSAGE SO CUSTOMERS LISTEN

- Go to mystorybrand.com and either create a BrandScript or log in to your existing BrandScript.
- Either alone or with a team, brainstorm empathetic statements you can make so your customers know you care about their internal problem.
- Brainstorm the many ways you can demonstrate competence and authority by exploring potential testimonials, statistics that demonstrate competence, awards you've won, or logos from other businesses you've helped succeed.
- Once you finish your brainstorming session, make the two StoryBrand BrandScript decisions that will allow you to fill out module 3.

AND MEETS A GUIDE

EMPATHY

_____
_____
_____

AUTHORITY

_____
_____
_____

CHAPTER 7

WHO GIVES THEM A PLAN

StoryBrand Principle Four: Customers
trust a guide who has a plan.

At this point in our customer's journey, we've identified
something they want, which got the story started. Then we
defined their problems, which created intrigue as to whether we
can help them overcome their challenges. Then we introduced
ourselves as the guide by expressing empathy and demonstrating
authority, which established trust. And yet, even with all this,
the customer isn't going to place an order. There's something
missing.

If we've positioned ourselves as the guide, our customers are
already in a relationship with us. But making a purchase isn't
a characteristic of a casual relationship; it's a characteristic of a
commitment. When a customer places an order, they're essentially saying, "I believe you can help me solve my problem, and

I believe it so much I'm willing to put skin in the game. I'm willing to part with my hard-earned dollars."

Commitments are risky for our customers because as soon as they make a commitment, they can lose something. Most customers are not going to take this risk yet.

When a customer is deciding whether to buy something, we should picture them standing on the edge of a rushing creek. It's true they want what's on the other side, but as they stand there, they hear a waterfall downstream. What happens if they fall into the creek? What would life look like if they went over those falls? These are the kinds of questions our customers subconsciously ponder as they hover their little arrow over the "Buy Now" button. *What if it doesn't work? What if I'm a fool for buying this?*

In order to ease our customers' concerns, we need to place large stones in that creek. When we identify the stones our customers can step on to get across the creek, we remove much of the risk and increase their comfort level about doing business with us. It's as though we're saying, "First, step here. See, it's easy. Then step here, then here, and then you'll be on the other side, and your problem will be resolved."

In the StoryBrand Framework, we refer to these "stones" as a *plan*.

In the movie *Moneyball*, Peter Brand (the guide) gives Billy Beane a plan he can employ to turn his baseball team around. In a series of steps, Billy will begin using an algorithm to choose players, rather than relying on anecdotal evidence from his antiquated coaching staff. He's going to begin to trust the numbers and run the team the way a hedge-fund manager might run his hedge fund.

In nearly every movie you can think of, the guide gives the

hero a plan. The plan is the bridge the hero must cross in order to arrive at the climactic scene. Rocky has to train using non-traditional methods, Tommy Boy has to embark on a national sales trip, and Juliet must drink the potion the apothecary gives her in order to trick her family into thinking she's died and to be free to be with Romeo.

The plan tightens the focus of the movie and gives the hero a "path of hope" she can walk that might lead to the resolution of her troubles.

THE PLAN CREATES CLARITY

Plans can take many shapes and forms, but all effective plans do one of two things: they either clarify how somebody can do business with us, or they remove the sense of risk somebody might have if they're considering investing in our products or services.

Remember the mantra "If you confuse, you lose"? Not having a plan is a guaranteed way to confuse your customers.

After potential customers listen to us give a keynote or visit our webpage or read an e-mail blast we've sent, they're all wondering the same thing: *What do you want me to do now?* If we don't guide them, they experience a little bit of confusion, and because they can hear that waterfall downstream, they use that confusion as an excuse not to do business with us.

The fact that we want them to place an order is not enough information to motivate them. If we're selling a storage system a customer can install in their garage, they hover over that "Buy Now" button subconsciously wondering whether it will work for them, how hard it will be to install, and whether it will sit unopened in the garage in boxes like the last thing they bought. But when we spell out how easy this whole thing is and let them know they can get started in three easy steps, they are more likely to place an order.

We must tell them to . . .

1. Measure your space.
2. Order the items that fit.
3. Install it in minutes using basic tools.

Even though these steps may seem obvious, they aren't obvious to our customers. Placing stones in the creek greatly increases the chance they will cross the creek.

THE PROCESS PLAN

At StoryBrand we've identified two plans you can use to effectively encourage customers to do business with you. The first kind of plan, and the one we recommend every one of our clients employ, is a process plan.

A process plan can describe the steps a customer needs to take to buy our product, or the steps the customer needs to take to use our product after they buy it, or a mixture of both.

For instance, if you're selling an expensive product, you might break down the steps like this:

1. Schedule an appointment.
2. Allow us to create a customized plan.
3. Let's execute the plan together.

Whether we're selling a financial product, a medical procedure, a university education, or any other complicated solution, a process plan takes the confusion out of our customer's journey and guides them in the next steps.

So far I've mostly talked about stones we can place in the creek that lead our customers to make a purchase, but another kind of process plan would be the post-purchase process plan. A post-purchase process plan is best used when our customers might have problems imagining how they would use our product after they buy it. For instance, with a complicated piece of software, we might want to spell out the steps or even the phases a customer would take after they make the purchase:

1. Download the software.
2. Integrate your database into our system.
3. Revolutionize your customer interaction.

The post-purchase process plan does the same thing a pre-purchase process plan does, in the sense that it alleviates confusion. When a customer is looking at the wide span between themselves and the integration of a complicated product, they're less likely to make a purchase. But when they read your plan, they think to themselves, *Oh, I can do that. That's not hard*, and they click "Buy Now."

A process plan can also combine the pre- and post-purchase steps. For instance:

1. Test-drive a car.
2. Purchase the car.
3. Enjoy free maintenance for life.

Again, the key to the success of *any* plan is to alleviate confusion for our customers. What steps do they need to take to do business with you? Spell out those steps, and it'll be as though you've paved a sidewalk through a field. More people will cross the field.

We get frequent questions about how many steps a process plan should have. The answer varies, of course, but we recommend at least three and no more than six. If doing business with you requires more than six steps, break down those steps into phases and describe the phases. In reality, you might guide your customer through twenty or thirty steps, but studies show when you bombard customers with information, buying decreases.

Remember, the whole point of creating a plan is to alleviate customers' confusion. Having more than four steps may actually add to, rather than reduce, confusion. The key is to simplify their journey so they are more likely to do business with you.

THE AGREEMENT PLAN

If process plans are about alleviating confusion, agreement plans are about alleviating fears.

An agreement plan is best understood as a list of agreements you make with your customers to help them overcome their fear of doing business with you.

Earlier I talked about CarMax and how they resolve the customer's agitation of having to deal with a used-car salesman. One of the tools they use to communicate that customers don't have to encounter this internal fear is an agreement plan. CarMax's four-point agreement includes the promise that customers will never have to haggle. Afraid you'll be stuck with a lemon? CarMax refuses to sell a car that doesn't meet their standards, and they put every car through a renewal process to be sure it earns their quality certification seal.[1]

Today, CarMax sells more cars than its next three competitors combined. In 2015, *Automotive News* named CarMax the undisputed used-car champion.[2] As I mentioned in chapter 5, CarMax rarely advertises the solution to their customers' external problems, that is, the need for a used car. Instead, they focus on their customers' internal problem, the fear of interacting with a used-car dealer, and they alleviate this fear with an agreement plan.

An agreement plan can also work to increase the perceived value of a service you promise to provide. For instance, Newt Gingrich's "Contract with America" is an example of an agreement plan. Newt was a relatively unknown congressman from Georgia who led a takeover in both houses of Congress by making an agreement with voters. Newt simply took age-old conservative talking points, turned them into a list, and said, "If you vote for us, we'll do all these things." More than three hundred conservative legislators signed on, and Newt became an overnight presidential hopeful.

Another benefit of an agreement plan is that it can work to clarify shared values between our customers and us. Whole Foods's list of values has attracted millions to their stores and, in ways, works as an agreement with their customers to source their food in a way that is socially and environmentally responsible.

Unlike a process plan, an agreement plan often works in the background. Agreement plans do not have to be featured on the home page of your website (though they could be), but as customers get to know you, they'll sense a deeper level to your service and may realize why when they finally encounter your agreement plan.

The best way to arrive at an agreement plan is to list all the things your customer might be concerned about as it relates to your product or service and then counter that list with agreements that will alleviate their fears.

If it's short enough (we're fans of brevity, obviously), you can feature your agreement plan on the wall of your business or even on your packaging or shopping bags.

WHAT'S THE PLAN CALLED?

Once you create your process or agreement plan (or both), consider giving them a title that will increase the perceived value of your product or service. For instance, your process plan might be called the "easy installation plan" or the "world's best night's sleep plan." Your agreement plan might be titled the "customer satisfaction agreement" or even "our quality guarantee." Titling your plan will frame it in the customer's mind and increases the perceived value of all that your brand offers.

Now that you've given your customer a plan, they will be much more likely to do business with you. You've lifted the fog, made things clear, set stones in the creek, and they are ready to continue the journey.

And yet before they'll make a commitment, they will need one more thing from you. They will need you to call them to action. I'll teach you the right and wrong ways to call customers to do business in the next chapter.

First, though, spend some time defining the plan or plans you want to implement to ease your customers' fears and concerns so they will engage your brand.

CLARIFY YOUR MESSAGE SO CUSTOMERS LISTEN

- Go to mystorybrand.com and either create a StoryBrand BrandScript or log in to your existing BrandScript.
- Either alone or with a team, brainstorm the simple steps a customer would need to take to do business with you (either a pre- or post-purchase process plan or a combination of both).
- What fears do your customers have related to your industry? What agreements could you make with them that would alleviate those fears? Feel free to use the notes feature of your BrandScript, where there is more room, to document your agreement plan. Use the plan section, then, to document the title of your plan.
- Do you share unique values with your customers? Can those values be spelled out in an agreement plan?
- Write the steps (and name) of your process plan on your StoryBrand BrandScript. If you're creating an agreement plan, simply use the notes section of your BrandScript to capture the agreement you'll be making with your customers.

WHO GIVES THEM A PLAN

PROCESS

_____

_____

_____

_____

AGREEMENT

_____

_____

_____

_____

CHAPTER 8

AND CALLS THEM TO ACTION

StoryBrand Principle Five: Customers do not take action unless they are challenged to take action.

At this point in our customers' story, they are excited. We've defined a desire, identified their challenges, empathized with their feelings, established our competency in helping them, and given them a plan. But they need us to do one more thing: they need us to call them to action.

ASK THEM TO PLACE AN ORDER

In stories, characters never take action on their own. They have to be challenged to take action. Tom Cruise's character would never have journeyed to pick up his brother in the movie *Rain*

Man unless he'd received a call explaining his father had died. Romeo wouldn't have climbed into the Capulet courtyard unless he'd fallen sick with love for Juliet. Elle Woods wouldn't have applied to Harvard unless she'd been dumped by her boyfriend. Liam Neeson's character wouldn't have chased the bad guys to Europe unless his daughter had been kidnapped.

The reason characters have to be challenged to take action is because everybody sitting in the dark theater knows human beings do not make major life decisions unless something challenges them to do so.

If I wrote a story about a guy who wanted to climb Everest and then one day looked at himself in the mirror and decided to do it, I'd lose the audience. That's not how people work. Bodies at rest tend to stay at rest, and so do customers. Heroes need to be challenged by outside forces.

Have you ever wondered why late-night infomercial hosts keep screaming, "Call now! Don't delay!" over and over as though they're trying to wake people up from a zombie trance? They do that because they're trying to wake people up from a zombie trance!

Your customers are bombarded with more than three thousand commercial messages per day, and unless we are bold in our calls to action, we will be ignored. If our calls to action are soft, they will not be noticed.

The Power of the "Buy Now" Button

I have a friend who has bought and sold nearly one hundred companies. He knows a lot about scaling a company up, and as he evaluates a company, he makes sure the people, products, and procedures are all healthy. But the key ingredient he looks for in a company is whether the company is challenging their customers to place orders. My friend knows the fastest way to grow a company is to make the calls to action clear and then repeat them over and over. He's made millions simply buying companies, creating stronger calls to action, and then selling the company after their revenue increases.

One of the biggest hindrances to business success is that we think customers can read our minds. It's obvious to us that we want them to place an order (why else would we be talking to them about our products?), so we assume it's obvious to them too. It isn't.

There should be a "Buy Now" button in the top right corner of your website, and it shouldn't be cluttered with a bunch of other buttons. The same call to action should be repeated above the fold and in the center of your website, and again and again as people scroll down the page.

Companies that don't make their calls to action clear remind me of my dating days before I met my wife. Instead of clearly asking a girl out, I'd say something like, "Coffee is nice, isn't it? Do you like coffee?"

What in the world is a woman supposed to do with a question like that? That's just not how you make a baby.

As I got older I realized the power of clarity. In fact, the way my wife and I got together was probably the clearest I've communicated about anything. I'd known Betsy from a distance for a while, but when I finally got up the courage to ask her out, I discovered she had a boyfriend. Still, I'd been passive long enough. I'd been hoping she'd notice how much I liked her even as I completely ignored her. It was time for a strong call to action. The next time I saw her, I told her how I really felt and that I'd like to call her in thirty days to ask her out. I said she'd need to ditch the other guy to keep things from being awkward.

Amazingly, thirty days later, she'd broken up with the other guy and we started dating. About a year later we got married. We're currently working on a baby that we're probably going to name "Buy Now" to remind everybody how important it is to have a clear call to action.

The moral of the story is people don't have ESP. They can't read our minds and they don't know what we want, even if it seems obvious. We have to clearly invite customers to take a journey with us or they won't.

When I was a kid there was a guy on late-night television who used to saw mattresses in half with a chainsaw. He'd scream at the camera that he'd gone crazy and was slashing prices on all kinds of furniture. I think a lot of us are afraid to ask for the sale because we don't want to look like that guy.

It's true we don't want to constantly beat our customers over the head with direct calls to action. Of the thousands of clients we've worked with, though, we've yet to encounter anybody who oversells. Most people think they're overselling when, in truth, their calls to action fall softer than a whisper.

Do You Believe in Your Product?

The reality is when we try to sell passively, we communicate a lack of belief in our product. When we don't ask clearly for the sale, the customer senses weakness. They sense we're asking for charity rather than to change their lives. Customers aren't looking for brands that are filled with doubt and want affirmation; they're looking for brands that have solutions to their problems.

If we can change our customer's story for the better, why

shouldn't we be bold about inviting them to do business with us? The guide in a movie must be direct with the hero about what they want the hero to do, otherwise the plot gets muddled and the audience starts to daydream.

Two Kinds of Calls to Action

At StoryBrand we recommend two kinds of calls to action: *direct calls to action* and *transitional calls to action*. They work like two phases of a relationship.

Let's say we ask a customer to buy but they don't. Who knows why, but they don't. There's no reason to end the relationship just because they aren't ready. I believe in honoring people who aren't ready, and I'm a fan of no-pressure sales. Still, I want to deepen the relationship so that whenever they need what I sell, they will remember me. The way I deepen that relationship is through transitional calls to action.

Direct calls to action include requests like "buy now," "schedule an appointment," or "call today." A direct call to action is something that leads to a sale, or at least is the first step down a path that leads to a sale.

Transitional calls to action, however, contain less risk and usually offer a customer something for free. Transitional calls to action can be used to "on-ramp" potential customers to an eventual purchase. Inviting people to watch a webinar or download a PDF are good examples of transitional calls to action.

To further the relational metaphor, a transitional call to action is like saying, "Can I take you out on a date?" to your customer, and a direct call to action is like saying, "Will you marry me?"

In our marketing collateral, we always want to have a direct call to action and a transitional call to action. The metaphorical conversation with our customers goes like this:

Us: Will you marry me?
Customer: No.
Us: Will you go out with me again?
Customer: Yes.
Us: Will you marry me now?
Customer: No.
Us: Will you go out with me again?
Customer: Sure, you're interesting and the information you provide is helpful.
Us: Will you marry me?
Customer: Okay, I'll marry you now.

As a brand, it's our job to pursue our customers. We want to get to know them and for them to get to know us, but we are the ones who need to take the initiative.

THOSE WHO ASK AGAIN AND AGAIN SHALL FINALLY RECEIVE

Years ago, I was preparing a keynote presentation for a global shampoo brand and my graphic designer was too busy with other projects to help. Not wanting to wait, I decided to outsource the presentation to a design house. I went looking online for a shop that dealt specifically with presentations and found two local houses that could help.

The first website I visited was beautifully designed—a

looping video loaded beneath text that explained the design house's values and priorities. After about twenty seconds admiring the look of their site, though, I started searching for information about how to do business with them. I couldn't find anything. They featured samples of previous projects, a few testimonials, and a phone number I could call but no direct, clear call to action. So I decided to check out their competitor's site.

The other company's site wasn't nearly as beautiful, but it dared to be clear. "If you're worried about a presentation, we can help you hit a grand slam." The truth is I was worried, and they spoke to my internal fear. They also painted a picture of a climactic scene: to hit a grand slam. Then they asked me out: they offered a PDF called "5 Things Great Presenters Get Right," and I was quite curious. I downloaded the PDF and read it in a few minutes. Their transitional call to action earned my trust and positioned them as the guide in my story. They had authority, it seemed. Then, on their website, they had a "schedule an appointment" button, and because they'd wined and dined me, I did. I never went back to the initial designer's website (which, remember, was much better looking), and before long I was gladly writing a check for several thousand dollars to the company that had clearly challenged me to take action.

Direct Calls to Action

It bears repeating: there should be one obvious button to press on your website, and it should be the direct call to action. When I say, "one obvious button," I don't mean "only one button," but rather one that stands out. Make the button a different color, larger, a bolder text, whatever you need to do. Then repeat that same button over and over so people see it as they scroll down the page.

Our customers should always know we want to marry them. Even if they're not ready, we should keep saying it. You just never know when they're going to want to make a commitment, and when they do, you want to be on one knee, holding flowers, smiling for the picture.

Examples of direct calls to action are

- Order now
- Call today
- Schedule an appointment
- Register today
- Buy now

Direct calls to action can be included at the end of every e-mail blast, on signage, in our radio ads, and even in our television commercials. Consider including direct calls to action in every team member's e-mail signature, and if you really want to get the point across, on all your business cards. The idea is to make it very clear what we'd like customers to do: to make a purchase so we can help them solve their problem.

Transitional Calls to Action

Direct calls to action are simple and obvious (though ridiculously underused), but transitional calls to action can be equally as powerful to grow your business. In fact, StoryBrand grew into a multimillion-dollar company in only its second year based solely on the use of a transitional call to action. Recognizing that most of our clients were using the StoryBrand Framework to fix their websites, we released a free PDF called "5 Things Your Website Should Include," and thousands of people downloaded it. At the back of the PDF we placed an ad for our StoryBrand Marketing Workshop. In the next twelve months, we doubled revenue without spending a dollar on marketing.

A good transitional call to action can do three powerful things for your brand:

1. **Stake a claim to your territory.** If you want to be known as the leader in a certain territory, stake a claim to that territory before the competition beats you to it. Creating a PDF, a video series, or anything else that positions you as the expert is a great way to establish authority.

2. **Create reciprocity.** I've never worried about giving away too much free information. In fact, the more generous a brand is, the more reciprocity they create. All relationships are give-and-take, and the more you give to your customers, the more likely they will be to give something back in the future. Give freely.

3. **Position yourself as the guide.** When you help your customers solve a problem, even for free, you position yourself as the guide. The next time they encounter a problem in that area of their lives, they will look to you for help.

Transitional calls to action come in all shapes and sizes. Here are a few ideas to create transitional calls to action of your own:

- **Free information:** Create a white paper or free PDF educating customers about your field of expertise. This will position you as a guide in your customer's story and create reciprocity. Educational videos, podcasts, webinars, and even live events are great transitional calls to action that on-ramp customers toward a purchase.

- **Testimonials:** Creating a video or PDF including testimonials from happy clients creates a story map in the minds of potential customers. When they see others experience a successful ending to their story, they will want that same ending for themselves.
- **Samples:** If you can give away free samples of your product, do it. Offering a customer the ability to test-drive a car, taste your seasoning, sample your music, or read a few pages of your book are great ways to introduce potential customers to your products.
- **Free trial:** Offering a limited-time free trial works as a risk-removal policy that helps to on-ramp your customers. Once they try your product, they may not be able to live without it.

Connecting the Dots

Earlier this year StoryBrand worked with a health clinic that specialized in health screening, drug testing, treating minor sicknesses, and giving shots. The primary traffic the clinic received was through businesses who needed their employees to complete drug tests. Still, the clinic was stagnant in growth. Customers were coming in to get one product but weren't aware of anything else the clinic offered.

Upon visiting the clinic, one of our StoryBrand Guides noticed they needed to create clear direct and transitional calls to action.

Patients would come into the shop, sign and date an entry form, then sit in the lobby reading magazines or watching television while they waited for a nurse. As one of our StoryBrand Certified Guides consulted with the clinic, she told the owner to remove the television and magazines. Instead of magazines, she encouraged them to create a transitional call to action called "The Healthy Body Checklist," allowing patients to self-assess their health. The checklist included questions like, "Do you feel tired at about two in the afternoon every day?" and "Are you satisfied with your current weight?" After patients finished their drug or blood tests, we suggested that nurses review the checklist with each patient and let them know about solutions that were also available at the clinic. The receptionist could then enter the customer's data into their e-mail marketing system and, based on how a patient was tagged, an automated campaign would go into effect. If the customer seemed like they needed more vitamin B, they'd get a series of e-mails explaining the benefits of a monthly vitamin B shot, along with clear calls to action directing the patient to make another appointment.

Is there a transitional call to action you can create that will grow your business? Are your direct calls to action clear and repeated often? If not, your customers likely don't know what you want them to do. Remember, people are drawn to clarity and away from confusion. Having clear calls to action means customers aren't confused about the actions they need to take to do business with you.

WHAT ARE THE STAKES?

Once customers decide to buy our products, how can we increase the perceived value of those products and deepen the positive experience they have with our brand? How can we make the story we've invited them into so enticing that they can't wait to turn the page?

To do this, we must define the stakes. What's at stake in the customer's story if they do or do not choose to do business with us? If we've not defined the stakes, we've not made the story interesting.

In the next two modules, I'll teach you how to deepen your customers' experience with your brand by defining exactly what's at stake.

Before we move forward, though, continue clarifying your business by brainstorming potential calls to action you can include in your StoryBrand BrandScript.

CLARIFY YOUR MESSAGE SO YOUR CUSTOMERS LISTEN

- Go to mystorybrand.com and either create a StoryBrand BrandScript or log in to your existing BrandScript.
- Decide what direct call to action you want to make obvious on all your marketing material.
- Brainstorm any transitional calls to action you can create that will stake a claim to your territory, create reciprocity with your customers, and position your brand as a guide.
- Fill out the "Call to Action" section of your StoryBrand BrandScript.

AND CALLS THEM TO ACTION

DIRECT

TRANSITIONAL

CHAPTER 9

THAT HELPS THEM AVOID FAILURE

StoryBrand Principle Six: Every human being is trying to avoid a tragic ending.

A story lives and dies based on the question: Will the hero succeed or will they fail? Throughout a story, storytellers foreshadow a potential successful ending and a potential tragic ending. The audience remains in suspense as long as the storyteller keeps the hero teetering on the precipice of success and failure.

The only two motivations a hero has in a story are to escape something bad or experience something good. Such is life. Our desire to avoid pain motivates us to seek a resolution to our problems.

If a storyteller doesn't clearly let an audience know what no-good, terrible, awful thing might befall their hero unless she overcomes her challenge, the story will have no stakes, and a story without stakes is boring.

As a rule, each scene in a movie must answer the question: What's at stake for the hero? Every conversation, every chase scene, every reflective montage should serve the movie in the same way: it must either move the character closer to, or further from, the tragic result that might befall them.

We kept turning the pages of Charlotte Brontë's *Jane Eyre* to find out the dark secret Edward Rochester had been hiding.

We sat on the edge of our seats in *Jaws* because we knew the citizens of Amity Island might be killed by the shark if Chief Martin Brody didn't do something.

Imagine a story in which nothing bad could befall the hero. Imagine a love story in which everything went well for the couple straight through to the beautiful and tension-free wedding. Imagine an action movie in which the bomb the hero had to destroy was actually a dud and nobody was in danger. Would an audience care?

Brands that don't warn their customers about what could happen if they don't buy their products fail to answer the "so what" question every customer is secretly asking.

WHERE'S THE MAYHEM?

Allstate Insurance's long-running Mayhem campaign features actor Dean Winters humorously portraying everything from raccoons in the attic to a raging fire started by a barbecue grill at a tailgating party. The idea was to humorously remind people why they needed insurance. Mayhem is always contrasted against the peaceful stability of Allstate, which asks the question, "Are you in good hands?"

In 2015, Allstate, along with the advertising agency Leo Burnett, took the campaign to a higher level. During the Sugar Bowl on New Year's Day, Allstate launched a campaign called Project Share Aware. The idea was to make people aware that sharing their whereabouts on social media might tip off criminals about when to burglarize their homes.

To announce the project, Allstate found a real couple and led them to believe they'd won a prize. They visited the couple in their home, secretly taking pictures of their household items. Later, they recreated their home on a soundstage, complete with duplicates of their belongings. The couple was then invited to attend the Sugar Bowl and given their own private box. During the game, Mayhem began auctioning off the couple's belongings on national television. People were directed to Mayhemsale.com for bargain-basement prices on everything from the couple's used car to an old tuba. As the couple watched their possessions being sold on the big screens at the game, they panicked. Hidden cameras caught their reactions and broadcast them on live television.

Of course, the couple's actual possessions were safe. Nevertheless, the campaign agitated a fear in many Americans. In fact, news outlets all over the country, including ABC News, *Wall Street Journal*, and the *New York Times*, covered the story. Suddenly, the threat of criminals walking into our homes as we announce our distant whereabouts on social media became a national fear.

The result? Mayhemsale.com received 6,000 to 10,000 hits per second immediately following each commercial. The site received more than 18 million hits during the game. Also, #Mayhemsale trended in the top ten hashtags during the game, and immediately after the commercials aired, surged to number one worldwide. Mayhem's Twitter followers increased by 24,000 during the game, and the first commercial of the campaign resulted in more than 20 million impressions on Facebook and almost 70,000 likes.[1] Allstate had, in the course of one football game, foreshadowed a potential failure for their customers and sold an insurance protecting them, both opening a story loop and offering to close it in a single campaign.

Of course, we don't all have access to the millions it takes to create a campaign like this, but the benefits of featuring the potential pitfalls of not doing business with us are much easier to include than we may think. Blog subjects, e-mail content, and bullet points on our website can all include elements of potential failure to give our customers a sense of urgency when it comes to our products and services.

WHAT'S THERE TO LOSE?

As it relates to our marketing, the obvious question is: What will the customer lose if they don't buy our products?

Some of you just cringed. I understand. I used to cringe when I thought about "warning" my customers about imminent doom too. Why wouldn't I? The last thing I want to be is a fearmonger, because it's true that fearmongers don't do well in the marketplace. But fearmongering is not the problem 99.9 percent of business leaders struggle with. Most of us struggle with the opposite. We don't bring up the negative stakes enough and so the story we're telling falls flat. Remember, if there are no stakes, there is no story.

People Are Motivated by Loss Aversion

Emphasizing potential loss is more than just good storytelling; it's good behavioral economics. In 1979, Nobel Memorial Prize winner Daniel Kahneman published a theory about why people make certain buying decisions. Prospect Theory, as it was called, espoused that people are more likely to be dissatisfied with a loss than they are satisfied with a gain. In other words, people hate losing $100 more than they like winning $100. This, of course, means loss aversion is a greater motivator of buying decisions than potential gains. In fact, according to Kahneman, in certain situations, people are two to three times more motivated to make a change to avoid a loss than they are to achieve a gain.[2]

When Lyndon Baines Johnson worked to pass the Civil Rights Act of 1964, he faced undying pressure from conservative political leaders across the South. One of the principal leaders who refused to endorse the legislation was George Wallace, then governor of Alabama. Wallace had no vote on the bill, but his influence threatened its passage all the same. At a crucial moment in the negotiations, Johnson sat Wallace down and explained he'd better get on the right side of history. Johnson said that Wallace's legacy hung in the balance, that they'd either build a statue in his honor or he'd be remembered for instigating hate. The choice was his. Johnson spelled out the narrative and emphasized the stakes, including the potential of the governor's tarnished legacy. The Civil Rights bill, of course, was passed.

So how do we use messages from the failure category in our marketing? In Dominic Infante, Andrew Rancer, and Deanna Womack's book *Building Communication Theory*, they propose a four-step process called a "fear appeal."

First, we must make a reader (or listener) know they are vulnerable to a threat. For example:

> "Nearly 30 percent of all homes have
> evidence of termite infestation."

Second, we should let the reader know that since they're vulnerable, they should take action to reduce their vulnerability.

> "Since nobody wants termites, you should do
> something about it to protect your home."

Third, we should let them know about a *specific* call to action that protects them from the risk.

> "We offer a complete home treatment that will
> insure your house is free of termites."

Fourth, we should challenge people to take this specific action.

> "Call us today and schedule your home treatment."[3]

Essentially, Infante, Rancer, and Womack present a soft way of agitating a fear and then highlight a path that would return readers or listeners to peace and stability.

Fear Is Salt in the Recipe

We do not need to use a great deal of fear in the story we're telling our customers. Just a pinch of salt in the recipe will do. While we do need to communicate something from the failure category in order to complete our BrandScript, too many warnings about imminent doom will turn customers off.

Infante, Rancer, and Womack explain why:

> When receivers are either very fearful or very unafraid, little attitude or behavior change results. High levels of fear are so strong that individuals block them out; low levels are too weak to produce the desired effect. Messages containing moderate amounts of fear-rousing content are most effective in producing attitudinal and/or behavior change.[4]

WHAT ARE YOU HELPING YOUR CUSTOMER AVOID?

What negative consequences are you helping customers avoid? Could customers lose money? Are there health risks if they avoid your services? What about opportunity costs? Could they make or save more money with you than they can with a competitor? Could their quality of life decline if they pass you by? What's the cost of not doing business with you?

If you're a financial advisor, for example, the list of what you're helping customers avoid might look like this:

- Confusion about how your money is being invested
- Not being ready for retirement
- A lack of transparency from your financial advisor
- A lack of one-on-one interaction with your advisor
- Hidden fees

We can even imagine a tragic scene that might befall our customers if they don't engage. Our financial advisor might write something like this:

"Don't postpone your retirement. You've worked too hard for too long to not enjoy time with your grandchildren."

Here are a few examples of what StoryBrand clients are helping their customers avoid:

PERKINS MOTORPLEX (USED CARS)

Getting ripped off by a used-car salesman
Being stuck with a lemon
Feeling taken advantage of

RELY TECHNOLOGY (AUDIO AND VIDEO FOR THE HOME)

Living in a boring home
Nobody will want to watch the game at your house
You need a PhD to turn on the TV

AEROSPACE MARKET ENTRY (MANUFACTURER OF AEROSPACE EQUIPMENT)

Product failure, damaging your reputation
Inefficient production
Being passed by the competition

WIN SHAPE CAMPS (SUMMER CAMP FOR KIDS)

A long, boring summer
A bunch of restless kids in your house
Regret about having wasted the summer

You can see how including these ideas in each client's marketing material will give their overall story a sense of completeness and urgency.

In this module of your StoryBrand BrandScript, you're only given a few bullet points. You'll notice you're given a great deal more in the success module. This, of course, is on purpose. You'll only need a few terrible, dastardly, awful things to warn your customers about to get the point across. Too much and your customers will resist you, too little and they won't know why your products even matter.

Once we've defined the stakes, your customers will be motivated to resist failure. Next we'll dramatically increase their motivation by helping them imagine what life can look like when they buy your products or services. After they see what you offer and how it can make their lives better, you'll have included stakes in the narrative and customer engagement will grow. First, though, let's warn customers about the consequences of not doing business with you.

CLARIFY YOUR MESSAGE SO CUSTOMERS LISTEN

- Go to mystorybrand.com and either create a StoryBrand BrandScript or log in to your existing BrandScript.
- Brainstorm the negative consequences you are helping your customers avoid.
- Write down at least three of those consequences on your
- StoryBrand BrandScript.

THAT HELPS THEM AVOID FAILURE

CHAPTER 10

AND ENDS IN A SUCCESS

StoryBrand Principle Seven: Never assume people understand how your brand can change their lives. Tell them.

Years ago, a friend gave me the best leadership advice I've ever received. He said, "Don, always remember, people want to be taken somewhere."

I've found that advice applies to my family, my team, the books I write, and the speeches I give. And it certainly applies to our marketing.

Where is your brand taking people? Are you taking them to financial security? To the day when they'll move into their dream home? To a fun weekend with friends? Without knowing it, every potential customer we meet is asking us where we can take them.

Ronald Reagan envisioned America as a shining city on a hill. Bill Clinton promised to build a bridge to the twenty-first

117

century. Casting a clear, aspirational vision has always served a presidential candidate.

By foreshadowing a potential successful ending to a story, or, as Stew Friedman at the Wharton School puts it, defining a "compelling image of an achievable future,"[1] leaders captivate the imaginations of their audiences.

Successful brands, like successful leaders, make it clear what life will look like if somebody engages their products or services. Nike promised to bring inspiration and innovation to every athlete. Likewise, Starbucks offered to inspire and nurture their customers, one cup at a time. For years, Men's Wearhouse promised, "You'll like the way you look," and they even guaranteed it.

Without a vision, the people perish. And so do brands.

In the final and most important element of the StoryBrand Framework, we're going to offer our customers what they want most: a happy ending to their story.

THE ENDING SHOULD BE SPECIFIC AND CLEAR

One of the problems we run into with StoryBrand clients is the vision they paint for their customer's future is too fuzzy. Nobody gets excited about a muddled vision. Stories aren't vague, they're defined; they're about specific things happening to specific people. Otherwise they're not stories; they're just lofty notions.

Harrison Ford had to defeat the terrorists on Air Force One to return to a peaceful White House. Erin Brockovich had to win the final verdict against Pacific Gas and Electric so the citizens of Hinkley, California, could know justice. In a good story, the resolution must be clearly defined so the audience knows exactly what to hope for.

Being specific matters. Kennedy would have bored the world had he cast a vision for a "highly competitive and productive space program." Instead, he defined the ambition specifically and as such inspired a nation: "We're going to put a man on the moon."

BEFORE AND AFTER

My friend Ryan Deiss at DigitalMarketer created a great tool to help us imagine the success our customers will experience if they use our products and services.

In a simple grid, Ryan allows us to see how our customers' lives will look after they engage us, how they will feel, what their average day will look like, and what kind of new status they will enjoy.

	BEFORE YOUR BRAND	AFTER YOUR BRAND
What do they have?		
What are they feeling?		
What's an average day like?		
What is their status?		

* From Ryan Deiss of Digital Marketer

Filling out this grid for your brand is a terrific exercise. Once you know how your customers' lives will change after they engage your brand, you will have plenty of copy to use in your marketing collateral.

The next step is to say it clearly. We must tell our customers what their lives will look like after they buy our products, or they will have no motivation to do so. We have to talk about the end vision we have for their lives in our keynotes, in our e-mail blasts, on our websites, and everywhere else.

Images are also important when it comes to casting a vision for our customers. If you're selling kitchen flooring, your website might show a happy mom picking up her child from the beautiful and sparkling kitchen floor. If you're selling education, show us students in the classroom having a great time learning in the environment you provide. Whatever it is you sell, show us people happily engaging with the product.

HOW TO END A STORY FOR YOUR CUSTOMER

Ultimately, the success module of your StoryBrand BrandScript should simply be a list of resolutions to your customers' problems. Brainstorm what your customer's life will look like externally if their problem is resolved, then think about how that resolution will make them feel, then consider why the resolution to their problem has made the world a more just place to live in. When we resolve our customers' internal, external, and philosophical problems, we've truly created a resolution that will satisfy their story.

If you want to take the concept a little deeper, it's worth exploring how most stories are resolved by story experts. Over the centuries, storytellers have learned what really gives an audience closure and a sense of satisfaction.

The three dominant ways storytellers end a story is by allowing the hero to

1. Win some sort of power or position.
2. Be unified with somebody or something that makes them whole.
3. Experience some kind of self-realization that also makes them whole.

The fact that these are the three most-employed story endings implies these are three dominant psychological desires shared by most human beings.

If our brand can promise a resolution that associates with one of these powerful desires, our BrandScript will be effective and our message will be enticing.

Let's explore the three desires more closely:

1. Winning Power and Position (The Need for Status)

When I was in high school, a film came out called *Can't Buy Me Love* in which a likable loser named Ronald Miller falls in love with a popular cheerleader named Cindy Mancini. Unfortunately for me, Ronald's character was so overlooked and invisible in his school that most people called him Donald. You can imagine the teasing I received.

But we loved the movie all the same. Why? Because in the

end, of course, Ronald gets the girl. But he gets more than the girl. He gains status. After winning the heart of Cindy, he becomes one of the popular kids, or, more accurately, he realizes trying to be somebody else is a waste of time, which, of course, makes him more popular.

Regardless, everybody wants status, which is evidenced by the number of "coming-of-age" stories in which a character realizes they've got what it takes to run with the big dogs.

As I mentioned earlier in the book, the primary function of our brain is to help us survive and thrive, and part of survival means gaining status. If our brand can participate in making our customers more esteemed, respected, and appealing in a social context, we're offering something they want.

So how can our brand offer status? There are many ways:

Offer access: My wife loves using her Starbucks membership card because it gains her points, which gains her status and the occasional free latte. We've had many conversations about the intangibility of said status, but I've learned not to argue. She's excited to be on her way to some kind of double-pump jazzy diamond level, which I'm pretty sure means she can cut in front of people at the drive-through.

Create scarcity: Offering a limited number of a specific item creates scarcity, and owning something that is scarce is often seen as a status symbol. When Jeep puts a badge that reads "limited" on the back of their Grand Cherokee, they're promoting the scarcity of the luxury SUV.

Offer a premium: Most companies earn 70 percent or more of their revenue from a small percentage of their clients. Few, though, identify those clients and offer them a title such as "Preferred" or "Diamond Member." I love being an "Emerald Club" member with National Car Rental because it means I get to bypass the counter, jump in a car, and drive off. We even recommend a status-associated title for the nonprofit brands we work with. People will be much more likely to donate if they know they are an "Anchor Donor" and even more likely if they get special privileges like updates from the founder or access to other anchor donors at fund-raisers.

Offer identity association: Premium brands like Mercedes and Rolex sell status as much as they do luxury. Is it worth it? Depends on who you ask. Status really does open doors, and by associating their brand, and thus their customers, with success and refinement, they offer them status.

2. Union That Makes the Hero Whole (The Need for Something External to Create Completeness)

The reason stories often end with the union of lovers has little to do with the desire for love or sex. Rather, union between male and female characteristics fulfills in the reader a desire for wholeness.

When the prince rescues the princess and they unite in a wedding at the end of the movie, the audience subconsciously experiences the joining of two halves. The subconscious idea is that the man needs to become more like a woman and the woman needs to become more like a man in order to be whole.

This need to be completed by an external source doesn't have to include a wedding or even a male or female character, however. A superhero deficient in a particular way could be helped out by another superhero who reenters the story at the end, for example.

The controlling idea of this kind of ending is that the character is rescued by somebody or something else that they needed in order for them to be made complete. In love stories, of course, it's all about the union of male and female characteristics, but the emotional need this kind of story resolves is much greater. It's about being made whole by external provision.

So what are some of the ways we can offer external help for customers looking to become complete or whole? Here are a few examples:

Reduced anxiety: For years, brands that sell basic items like dish detergent and glass cleaner have almost comically positioned their products as anti-anxiety medication. As the hero in the commercial uses the product, his or her sense of frustration subsides until, at last, they're able to see their bright shining face glowing back at them in the polished platter, and then off they go into the sunset. What is the brand really offering? Satisfaction for a job well done. A feeling of closure about a clean house. A better, more peaceful life. Will the use of your product lead to the relief of stress and a feeling of completeness? If so, talk about it and show it in your marketing material.

Reduced workload: Customers who don't have the right tools must work harder because they are, well, incomplete. But what if a tool you offer could give them what they're missing? Whether they're selling wheelbarrows, software, jackhammers, or a fishing apparatus, manufacturers have been positioning tools as "the thing that will make you superhuman" for decades.

AND ENDS IN A SUCCESS

More time: For many customers, time is the enemy, and if our product can expand time, we're offering to solve an external problem that is causing an internal frustration. Not being able to "fit it all in" is often perceived by our customers as a personal deficiency. Any tool, system, philosophy, or even person who can expand time may offer a sense of completeness.

3. Ultimate Self-Realization or Acceptance (The Need to Reach Our Potential)

Movies like *Rudy*, *Hoosiers*, and *Chariots of Fire* all tap into the human desire to reach our potential. And it's not just sports movies. *Legally Blonde*, *The Theory of Everything*, and *Whiplash* are all about heroes who face great odds in their journey to prove themselves. Once proven, the heroes realize an inner peace and can finally accept themselves because they've reached their potential.

An outward demonstration of worth isn't always necessary to create this kind of resolution. Heroes can also take an internal journey to come to the same conclusion. When Bridget Jones realized she was too good for the boss with whom she desired a relationship, she came to an ultimate self-realization that returned her to a place of peace and stability. And while it's true she didn't close the story loop of uniting with the man she wanted, resolution is brought about as she abandons that goal in exchange for the greater fulfillment of self-acceptance and contentment.

In 2013, the soap company Dove released a series of short films featuring women who were the subjects of an FBI-trained forensic artist. Without actually seeing the women, the artist would draw each woman based on how she described herself. Later, the artist would draw the same woman based on how a stranger described her. The reveal was shocking. The sketches drawn from the stranger's description were always more beautiful than the ones in which the women described themselves. The point: many women don't realize how beautiful they are. The ad was an attempt to help women accept themselves and find greater contentment in their intrinsic beauty.

Whether it's by fulfilling some purpose or accepting themselves as they are, this return to contentment resolves something in a story that is universally human: the desire for self-acceptance.

How can a brand offer a sense of ultimate self-realization or self-acceptance? Here are a few ideas:

Inspiration: If an aspect of your brand can offer or be associated with an inspirational feat, open the floodgates. Brands like Red Bull, *Harvard Business Review*, Under Armour, The Ken Blanchard Company, Michelob Ultra, and even GMC have associated themselves with athletic and intellectual accomplishment and thus a sense of self-actualization.

Acceptance: Helping people accept themselves as they are isn't just a thoughtful thing to do; it's good marketing. Not unlike the Dove campaign, American Eagle turned heads when they launched their Aerie campaign. In the campaign, American Eagle used real people as models and refused to retouch the images. Tackling body-image issues, American Eagle went beyond basic product promotion and contributed to universal self-acceptance among their clientele.

Transcendence: Brands that invite customers to participate in a larger movement offer a greater, more impactful life along with their products and services. Tom's Shoes built a name for itself by selling stylish shoes while simultaneously giving a pair to somebody in need in what they called a "one for one" model. Those who wore the shoes claimed a major factor in deciding to make the purchase was a sense of involvement with a larger movement. At less than ten years old, the for-profit brand sold for more than $700 million. Another example of a brand that helps customers achieve a level of transcendence is Daymond John's clothing brand FUBU, an acronym for "For Us By Us," in reference to the African American community being represented in the marketplace. The brand offers more than fashion; it offers a sense of unity, transcendence, and entrepreneurialism for the African American community.

CLOSING THE STORY LOOPS

The idea behind the success module in the SB7 Framework is that we offer to close a story loop. Human beings are looking for resolutions to their external, internal, and philosophical problems, and they can achieve this through, among other things, status, self-realization, self-acceptance, and transcendence. If our products can help people achieve these things, we should make this a core aspect of our brand promise.

KEEP IT SIMPLE

Offering to close a story loop is much more simple than you think. Even the inclusion of smiley, happy people on your website is a strong way to offer the closing of a story loop. People want to be happy, and those images promise your product will deliver.

If you sell rugs, a successful resolution might be a beautiful floor or a room that finally feels finished. If you sell ice cream, a successful resolution might be a rich, creamy taste of heaven. Camping gear? An adventure to remember.

While I've been slightly philosophical in this chapter, try not to overthink it. What problem are you resolving in your customer's life, and what does that resolution look like? Stick to basic answers because basic answers really do work. Then, when you get good, start diving deeper into the levels of problems your brand resolves.

The important idea in this section is that we need to show repeatedly how our product or service can make somebody's life better. If we don't tell people where we're taking them, they won't follow. A story has to go somewhere.

Have you told your customers where you want to take them?

CLARIFY YOUR MESSAGE SO CUSTOMERS LISTEN

- Go to mystorybrand.com and either create a StoryBrand BrandScript or log in to your existing BrandScript.
- Brainstorm the successful resolution you're helping your customers achieve. What will their lives look like if they use your products and services?
- Use the bullet points in the success module of your BrandScript to capture your best answers.

Now that you've created your StoryBrand BrandScript, let's take a look at the biggest motivator your customer has for making a purchase: the desire to become somebody different.

THAT ENDS IN A SUCCESS

CHAPTER 11

PEOPLE WANT YOUR BRAND TO PARTICIPATE IN THEIR TRANSFORMATION

Even though you've filled out all seven parts of your StoryBrand BrandScript, you've likely noticed there's one left. The final section serves as the foundation for the overall BrandScript and will help you create a guiding focus for your brand. In fact, we've only danced around the greatest single motivation your customer has. This single motivator is the driving force behind nearly every decision we make as human beings. Whether we're buying lawn furniture or choosing a mate, we can't escape it.

I'm talking about the human desire to *transform*.

Everybody wants to change. Everybody wants to be somebody different, somebody better, or, perhaps, somebody who simply becomes more self-accepting.

When you look closely at your BrandScript, you'll see it. Your brand is helping people become better versions of themselves, which is a beautiful thing. You are helping them become wiser, more equipped, more physically fit, more accepted, and more at peace. Like it or not (and we hope you like it), we are all participating in our customers' transformation, which is exactly what they want us to do.

Brands that participate in the identity transformation of their customers create passionate brand evangelists.

HEROES ARE DESIGNED TO TRANSFORM

At the beginning of a story, the hero is usually flawed, filled with doubt, and ill-equipped for the task set before them. The guide aids them on their journey, rife with conflict. The conflict begins to change the character, though. Forced into action, the hero develops skills and accrues the experience needed to defeat their foe. Though the hero is still filled with doubt, they summon the courage to engage, and in the climactic scene defeat the villain, proving once and for all they have changed, that they are now competent to face challenges and are better versions of themselves. The story has transformed them.

This same character arc, by the way, is the arc for *The Old Man and the Sea*, *Pride and Prejudice*, *Pinocchio*, *Hamlet*, *Sleeping Beauty*, and *Tommy Boy*. It's the arc of almost every popular story we can name. Why? Because it's our story. Feelings of self-doubt are universal, as is the desire to become somebody competent and courageous. And all of this matters when it comes to branding our products and services.

A few important questions we have to ask ourselves when we're representing our brand are: Who does our customer want to become? What kind of person do they want to be? What is their aspirational identity?

SMART BRANDS DEFINE AN ASPIRATIONAL IDENTITY

Recently I ran down to Home Depot to get a stud finder so I could install shelving in the garage. Next to the stud finders in the tool section was a selection of Gerber Knives. Gerber is a knife company out of Portland, Oregon, that makes a range of multipurpose pocketknives. Their commercial campaign, however, offers the buyer a lot more than a knife. They sell something intangible. They sell an identity, and by that I mean they sell a kind of person you and I can become. I'd been studying their commercials for a long time, and even though I knew exactly what they were doing to my subconscious, I wanted one anyway. *But why?* I thought to myself as I stood there staring at the knives. *I'm a writer. The only thing I need a knife for is to make a peanut butter and jelly sandwich.*

Still, the pull was palpable. What if I had to swim under a boat to cut a tangled rope from its propeller? Or cut a pant leg off my bloody blue jeans to make a tourniquet for my injured arm?

Thankfully my executive brain overpowered my primitive brain and I walked away with just the stud finder. But why was it so hard? Why did I want the knife so badly? And then why did I specifically want a Gerber Knife? Certainly they make great knives, but there are many other companies making great knives and I'd never really cared or noticed.

The reason was simple. Gerber defined an aspirational identity for their customers and they associated their product with that identity. The aspirational identity of a Gerber Knife customer is that they are tough, adventurous, fearless, action oriented, and competent to do a hard job. Epitomized in their advertising campaign "Hello Trouble," Gerber positioned their customer as the kind of person who sails boats into storms, rides bulls, rescues people from floods, and yes, cuts tangled ropes from boat propellers. In their television commercials they present images of these aspirational, heroic figures over anthemic music and a narrator reciting the lines:

> Hello, Trouble.
> It's been awhile since we last met.
> But I know you're still out there.
> And I have a feeling you're looking for me.
> You wish I'd forget you, don't you, Trouble?
> Perhaps it's you that has forgotten me.
> Perhaps I need to come find you,
>   remind you who I am.[1]

The commercial is terrific. One day, to my surprise, a StoryBrand alumnus, who happened to have been one of the Army Rangers about whom the movie *Black Hawk Down* was made, stopped by the house. We caught up for a moment, and then he gave me a little thank-you present, a Gerber Knife. He even had my name engraved on the blade. He knew I liked the commercial and thought it would be a thoughtful gift. To this day I keep that knife clipped to the dashboard of my truck. Occasionally I'll take it into the kitchen, stare at a jar of peanut butter, and say, "Hello, Trouble."

I may just be a writer, but I love that knife.

But let me ask you a question. Was that knife a waste of money? I mean, let's say I did pay forty dollars for the knife and never used it. Did I get ripped off?

I've asked that question to hundreds of people who've attended the StoryBrand Marketing Workshop, and the answer has always come back the same: no. It was not a waste of money. It was well worth the forty dollars. I can't help but agree. The truth is I got a knife and something more than a knife. In a way, Gerber helped me become a better person. They defined an aspirational identity and invited me to step into it. They made me feel more tough and adventurous, and they even created a moment between two friends. And that's worth a great deal more than forty dollars.

HOW DOES YOUR CUSTOMER WANT TO BE DESCRIBED BY OTHERS?

The best way to identify an aspirational identity that our customers may be attracted to is to consider how they want their friends to talk about them. Think about it. When others talk about you, what do you want them to say? How we answer that question reveals who it is we'd like to be.

It's the same for our customers. As it relates to your brand, how does your customer want to be perceived by their friends? And can you help them become that kind of person? Can you participate in their identity transformation? If you offer executive coaching, your clients may want to be seen as competent, generous, and disciplined. If you sell sports equipment, your customers likely want to be perceived as active, fit, and successful in their athletic pursuits.

Once we know who our customers want to be, we will have language to use in e-mails, blog posts, and all manner of marketing material.

A GUIDE OFFERS MORE THAN A PRODUCT AND A PLAN

Playing the guide is more than a marketing strategy; it's a position of the heart. When a brand commits itself to their customers' journey, to helping resolve their external, internal, and philosophical problems, and then inspires them with an aspirational identity, they do more than sell products—they change lives. And leaders who care more about changing lives than they do about selling products tend to do a good bit of both.

Last year StoryBrand consulted with Dave Ramsey and his team at Ramsey Solutions. Ramsey Solutions may be the best example of a narrative-based company I know, and Dave himself is a terrific example of a guide. Over a series of workshops, dinners, and speeches, we introduced the Ramsey team to the SB7 Framework, less as a way of educating them than as a way of giving vocabulary to what they were already doing.

Dave Ramsey hosts one of the largest radio shows in America with more than eight million daily listeners. On the show he offers financial advice and strategies that center around tackling and conquering personal debt. Unlike many advisors, though, Ramsey offers more than wisdom; he offers a narrative map his customers can enter into. Ramsey comes back from every break on his radio show with the same line: "Welcome back to *The Dave Ramsey Show*, where debt is dumb, cash is king, and the paid-off home mortgage has taken the place of the BMW as the status symbol of choice." There they are, the elements of story, complete with an identity to step into and a new status symbol to go along with it.

Though Dave's face is prominent on book covers and billboards promoting his show, he never positions himself as the hero. Instead, Ramsey has a near obsession with his listeners' journeys. Dave's understanding of his listeners' external problems (consumer debt and financial illiteracy), internal problems (confusion and a feeling of hopelessness), as well as their philosophical problem (accruing debt for things we don't need posits moral questions) engages listeners in a living story. Always entertaining, Dave never misses an opportunity to embolden his listeners with an aspirational identity, encourage their improvements, and remind them that tackling their financial challenges is a step to personal strength and there are few of life's problems that can't be conquered with a little strategy and commitment.

Dave even offers a climactic scene in his customers' story. After executing a plan he offers through his Financial Peace University, listeners are invited on his show to perform a "Debt-Free Scream." People travel from thousands of miles away to be featured on the show, and when they arrive, dozens of the Ramsey team surround the accomplished hero with applause as the hero shouts, "I'm debt-free!"

Once a listener has completed the journey, Dave lets them know they've changed, that they're different now and there's nothing they can't accomplish if they apply themselves.

GREAT BRANDS OBSESS ABOUT THE TRANSFORMATION OF THEIR CUSTOMERS

When we first met with Dave, I was surprised to learn he didn't know that affirming the hero's transformation was an oft included scene at the end of many stories. After the climactic scene (the debt-free scream), the guide comes back to affirm the transformation of the hero.

In *Star Wars*, the ghost of Obi-Wan stands next to Luke Skywalker as he's rewarded for bravery. In *The King's Speech*, Lionel tells King George he will be a great king. Peter Brand sits Billy Beane down in the movie *Moneyball* and lets him know he's hit the equivalent of a home run as the manager of the A's.

The main purpose these scenes serve is to mark the transformation the hero has experienced so the audience has a point of reference that contrasts the hero's character from the story's beginning. The audience needs to be told very clearly how far the hero has come, especially since the hero usually struggles with crippling doubt right up until the end and they don't even realize how much they have changed.

A hero needs somebody else to step into the story to tell them they're different, they're better. That somebody is the guide. That somebody is you.

There are hundreds of thousands of financial advisors, and thousands of them have written books. Hundreds of those who've written books have podcasts or radio shows, and yet Dave Ramsey enjoys a wider popularity. Why? Well, certainly his advice is good. Nobody is attracted to incompetence. But I'm convinced it is the way he frames the customer's journey as a narrative and participates in their transformation that sets him apart.

IDENTITY TRANSFORMATION

In the foundational module of your StoryBrand BrandScript, we've included a section that will allow you to define an identity transformation your customer may experience as they relate to your brand.

Who does your customer want to become as they relate to your products and services?

At StoryBrand, we want our customers to become marketing experts. When they leave our workshop or after having spent time with one of our StoryBrand Guides, we want them to return to the office and have people wondering what happened to them. How did they get such marketing savvy? How did they become so clear in their thinking? Why are their ideas suddenly so good? Did they suddenly get a PhD in messaging?

Similar to the success module of your BrandScript, the aspirational identity section answers a question about how the story ends, except instead of telling us where the story is going, it tells us who the hero has become.

Brands that realize their customers are human, filled with emotion, driven to transform, and in need of help truly do more than sell products; they change people. Dave Ramsey changes people. Starbucks changes people. Apple changes people. Tom's Shoes changes people. Gerber Knives changes people. It's no wonder brands like these have such passionate fans and do so well in the marketplace.

EXAMPLES OF IDENTITY TRANSFORMATION

Thousands of StoryBrand clients have defined an aspirational identity for their customers and begun to participate in their transformation. Because of this, more and more companies are not just improving the world through their products and services; they're actually improving the way their customers see themselves. Offering an aspirational identity to our clients adds enormous value to everything else that we offer.

Here are some examples of aspirational identities from StoryBrand alumni:

PET FOOD BRAND

From: Passive dog owner
To: Every dog's hero

FINANCIAL ADVISOR

From: Confused and ill-equipped
To: Competent and smart

SHAMPOO BRAND

From: Anxious and glum
To: Carefree and radiant

Have you thought about who you want your customer to become? Participating in your customer's transformation can give new life and meaning to your business. When your team realizes that they sell more than products, that they guide people toward a stronger belief in themselves, then their work will have greater meaning.

Spend some time thinking about who you want your customers to become. How can you improve the way they see themselves?

How can your brand participate in your customer's transformational journey?

Let's do more than help our heroes win; let's help them transform.

CLARIFY YOUR MESSAGE SO CUSTOMERS LISTEN

- Go to mystorybrand.com and either create a StoryBrand BrandScript or log in to your existing BrandScript.
- Brainstorm the aspirational identity of your customer. Who do they want to become? How do they want to be perceived by others?
- Use the "to" lines of your BrandScript to define an aspirational identity. Filling out the "from" line is then simple. It's simply the opposite of whatever you define as their aspirational identity captured in the "to" line.

CHARACTER TRANSFORMATION	
FROM	TO

IMPLEMENTING YOUR STORYBRAND BRANDSCRIPT

CHAPTER 12

BUILDING A BETTER WEBSITE

We will only see an increased engagement from customers if we implement our StoryBrand BrandScript in our marketing and messaging material. The BrandScript you've put together has to show up on websites, in e-mail campaigns, elevator pitches, and sales scripts. You must edit existing marketing materials and create new and better materials, then get those materials in the hands of potential customers.

To the degree that you implement your StoryBrand BrandScript is the degree to which people will understand why they need your products. The more we implement, the more customers will listen.

The more you execute, the more clearly you'll communicate and the more your brand will stand out.

The third section of *Building a StoryBrand* gives both large and small companies tangible, practical steps they can take to apply their StoryBrand BrandScript. Whether you're a mom-and-pop shop, a start-up, a personal brand, or even a multibillion-dollar organization, you'll learn from the thousands of companies who have created and executed their StoryBrand BrandScript to see radical results.

START WITH YOUR WEBSITE

Most of us don't have millions to spend on a marketing campaign, but that's okay. These days we can get serious traction just paying attention to our digital presence. A great digital presence starts with a clear and effective website. Our website isn't the only tool we need to motivate buyers, but it's usually the one that does the heavy lifting. People may hear about us through word of mouth or social media, but they definitely go to our website to learn more. When they get to our website, their "hopes need to be confirmed," and they need to be convinced we have a solution to their problem.

In short, we need a website that passes the grunt test and converts browsers into buyers.

KEEP IT SIMPLE

At our workshops we've reviewed thousands of websites, and most of them have succumbed to villainous noise. The days of using our website as a clearinghouse of information are over. Businesses were once able to post all the small print about what they do on their website, but the Internet has changed. Today your website should be the equivalent of an elevator pitch.

Your website is likely the first impression a potential customer will receive about your company. It's almost like a first date. The customer simply needs to know that you have something they want and you can be trusted to deliver whatever that is.

Even if your company has grown because of word of mouth, a website full of noise can kill potential sales. Your website matters.

As we've helped our clients create great websites, we've come back to five things they need to include in order to see results. These five things are just the beginning of a marketing campaign, but unless we've got these five things working for us, there's no reason to move on. Let's just call these the basics.

THE FIVE THINGS YOUR WEBSITE SHOULD INCLUDE

1. An Offer Above the Fold

When people go to your website, the first thing they see is the images and text above the fold. The term *above the fold* comes from the newspaper industry and refers to the stories printed above where the newspaper folds in half. On a website, the images and text above the fold are the things you see and read before you start scrolling down.

As I mentioned earlier, I like to think of the messages above the fold as a first date, and then as you scroll down you can put the messages you want to share on a second and third date. But as we've talked about, the stuff you share on a first date should be short, enticing, and exclusively customer-centric.

My wife was recently gifted an online membership to some sort of cooking school in Seattle. A friend sent it to her as a thank-you for some work she'd done on their website. At first, Betsy was excited, until she went to the site. On the main page of the site (before she logged in), there was a beautiful picture of a carrot cake and beneath it some kind of inside joke about having something to eat while watching *Game of Thrones*. We didn't get it. She scrolled down and clicked on a video, hoping it would explain what kind of thing she'd been given. Instead, the video featured a cartoon explanation of how the company got started. Somebody named Joe met somebody named Karen, who was friends with somebody named Todd, and they all loved cooking!

It wasn't until my wife signed in and began exploring what the site offered that she got excited. She came to bed that night telling me about a certain kind of natural ingredient she could use to take the color out of liquor so all her cocktails would look clear. I didn't understand why this was important until she explained that the sage from her garden would stand out more as it hung from the glass. "Oh, the sage," I said. "They offer a service to help your sage stand out."

"No," Betsy said. "It took me a couple hours to figure it out, but the whole subscription is about these three fun friends in Seattle who are going to make me a pro in the kitchen!"

BINGO! Betsy said it. She said the very words that needed to be printed above the fold on their website:

"WE WILL MAKE YOU A PRO IN THE KITCHEN!"

One short sentence would have helped us understand what they offered and even given us words to use to help their business spread.

There is no telling how many customers that site is losing because they are making their customers work so hard to understand why anybody would need their service. My own wife, who now loves the site, would have bounced had she not been given a free pass.

The idea here is that customers need to know what's in it for them right when they read the text. The text should be bold and the statement should be short. It should be easy to read and not buried under buttons and clutter. I recently went to the website for Squarespace and it simply said, "We Help You Make Beautiful Websites." Perfect. They could have said a lot of things on their website, but because they know to keep messages short and relevant, they're making millions.

Above the fold, make sure the images and text you use meet one of the following criteria:

- They promise an aspirational identity.

  By offering to make my wife a pro in the kitchen, the school in Seattle could have let her know "what's in it for her" by appealing to an aspirational identity. Can we help our customers become competent in something? Will they be different people after they've engaged us? Let's spell it out clearly.

- They promise to solve a problem.

  If you can fix a problem, tell us. Can you stop my cat from clawing the furniture? My car from overheating? My hair from thinning? Say it. We didn't go to your website to read about how many company softball games you've won; we came here to solve a problem.

- They state exactly what they do.

  The easiest thing we can do on our website is state exactly what we do. There's a shop down the street from us called Local Honey, which would cause anybody to think they sell local honey. They quickly overcame this confusion, though, with a tagline that says, "We sell clothes. We do hair." Gotcha. Local Honey sells clothes and does hair. I've now filed them away in the Rolodex of my brain and will remember them when I need new hair or new clothes.

Take a look at your website and make sure it's obvious what you can offer a customer. Some of our clients do spell out their offer, but they spell it out in the middle of a paragraph that starts out, "We've been in business since 1979, committed to excellence and caring about our customers . . ." That's all nice and sweet, but J. K. Rowling didn't start her first Harry Potter novel with "My name is J. K. Rowling and for a long time I've wanted to write a book . . ." The fact that she always wanted to write a book wasn't part of the actual Harry Potter story, and she was smart enough to know it. She got straight to the point. She hooked the reader. She was smart, and we can be smart too. An offer above the fold is a sure way to get a customer hooked on the story we're telling.

2. Obvious Calls to Action

If you're not sure what a call to action is, go back and read chapter 8 in this book. It's important. For now, know that the whole point of your website is to create a place where the direct call to action button makes sense and is enticing. While we're in business to serve our customers and better the world, we'll be out of business soon if people don't click that "Buy Now" button. Let's not hide it.

There are two main places we want to place a direct call to action. The first is at the top right of our website and the second is in the center of the screen, above the fold. Your customer's eye moves quickly in a Z pattern across your website, so if the top left is your logo and perhaps tagline, your top right is a "Buy Now" button, and the middle of the page is an offer followed by another "Buy Now" button, then you've likely gotten through all the noise in your customer's mind and they know what role you can play in their story.

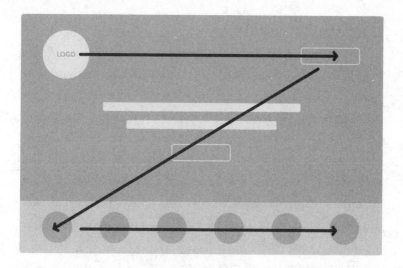

For best results the "Buy Now" buttons should be a different color from any other button on the site (preferably brighter so it stands out), and both buttons should look exactly the same. I know this sounds like overkill, but remember, people don't read websites, they scan them. You want that button to keep showing up like a recurring theme. A person has to hear something (or read something) many times before they process the information, so we want to repeat our main call to action several times.

Your transitional call to action should also be obvious, but don't let it distract from the direct call to action. I like featuring the transitional call to action in a less-bright button next to the call to action so the "Will you marry me?" and "Can we go out again?" requests are right next to each other. Remember, if you aren't asking people to place an order, they won't.

[BUY NOW] [DOWNLOAD PDF]

3. Images of Success

Words make up the majority of our messaging, but not all of it. The images we use on our websites also communicate something. If people come to our website and see pictures of our building, we're likely wasting some of their mental bandwidth on meaningless messages, unless, of course, you're a bed-and-breakfast. But even then, images of the building aren't what I'd lead with. I'd save that for the second date. We believe images of smiling, happy people who have had a pleasurable experience (closed an open story loop) by engaging your brand should be featured on your website.

Everybody wants to experience a better life in some way or another, and while it may seem simple, images of people smiling or looking satisfied speak to us. They represent an emotional destination we'd like to head toward.

Many of us need to display our products, but if we can feature those products in the hands of smiling people, our images might have more power. Not everybody needs to be smiling, of course; this wouldn't seem authentic. But in general we need to communicate a sense of health, well-being, and satisfaction with our brand. The easiest way to do this is by displaying happy customers.

4. A Bite-Sized Breakdown of Your Revenue Streams

A common challenge for many businesses is that they need to communicate simply about what they do, but they've diversified their revenue streams so widely that they're having trouble knowing where to start. If this is your struggle, you're hardly alone. We had a client a couple of years ago that had two main products: a two-day personalized life-planning process for individuals and a two-day strategic operations planning session for teams of executive leaders. Sounds simple enough, except the company didn't really make money off either product; instead, they made money training and certifying the facilitators. The challenge, then, was to increase demand for each product so that more people would want to become facilitators. This means they had to drive traffic to three different products: the life-planning product, the strat-ops product, and the facilitator certification.

If this company sounds like yours, the first challenge is to find an overall umbrella message that unifies your various streams. For our friends delivering life-planning and strat-ops facilitation, we chose the need people have for a customized plan. Above the fold on their website, we recommended the text "The Key to Success Is a Customized Plan" over an image of a facilitator mapping out a plan on a whiteboard for a satisfied client. As potential customers scrolled down the page, they would see two sections to choose from, personal life plans and corporate strategy plans. Each of these buttons led to new pages with messages filtered by two different BrandScripts. Customers were able to schedule facilitations on either page. The key to growing the business, though, was a button at the top and bottom of each and every page that said, "Become a Trained Facilitator."

We may think our business is too diverse to communicate clearly, but it probably isn't. Certainly there are examples where various brands within an umbrella company need to be split up and marketed separately, but in most cases we can find an umbrella theme to unite them all. Once we have an umbrella message, we can separate the divisions using different web pages and different BrandScripts. The key is clarity. When we break down our divisions clearly so people can understand what we offer, customers will be able to choose their own adventure without getting lost.

5. Very Few Words

People don't read websites anymore; they scan them. If there is a paragraph above the fold on your website, it's being passed over, I promise. Around the office we use the phrase "write it in Morse code" when we need marketing copy. By "Morse code" we mean copy that is brief, punchy, and relevant to our customers. Think again about our caveman sitting in his cave. "You sell cupcakes. Cupcakes good. Me want eat cupcake. Me like pink one and must go to bakery now." Most of us err too far in the opposite direction. We use too much text.

Why say, "As parents ourselves, we understand what it feels like to want the best for our children. That's why we've created a school where parents work closely with teachers through every step of their child's education journey," when you could just say, "Weekly Conference Calls with Your Child's Teacher" as a bullet point along with five other great differentiators about your school?

As customers scroll down your page, it's okay to use more and more words, but by more and more I really mean a few sentences here and there. Some of the most effective websites I've reviewed have used ten sentences or less on the entire page. That's the equivalent of about ten tweets or one press conference with Bill Belichick.

If you do want to use a long section of text to explain something (we do it on our site, in fact), just place a little "read more" link at the end of the first or second sentence so people can expand it if they like, that way you aren't bombarding customers with too much text.

As an experiment, let's see if you can cut half the words out of your website. Can you replace some of your text with images? Can you reduce whole paragraphs into three or four bullet points? Can you summarize sentences into bite-sized soundbites? If so, make those changes soon. The rule is this: the fewer words you use, the more likely it is that people will read them.

STAY ON SCRIPT

These are the five most important things to do with your website. There are more, of course, but if you added all the rest of the tips and strategies together, they wouldn't make as big of a difference as getting these five things right.

If you think about your StoryBrand BrandScript as a drum kit, think of your website as a drum solo. There shouldn't be a single word, image, or idea shared on your website that doesn't come from the thoughts generated by your StoryBrand BrandScript. The words don't have to be an exact replica of your

BrandScript, but the ideas should be the same. If you're including messages on your website that don't come from one of the categories of the StoryBrand 7-Part Framework, your customers will only hear noise.

THIRTEEN

USING STORYBRAND TO TRANSFORM COMPANY CULTURE

So far we've seen how a solid StoryBrand BrandScript transforms *customer* engagement. But its value doesn't stop there. Your BrandScript can also be leveraged to transform *employee* engagement. And that has enormous implications for your company culture.

Customers aren't the only ones who get confused when the message is unclear. Employees get confused too, from the division president to the regional manager to the laborer earning minimum wage on the front line.

THE CURSE OF THE NARRATIVE VOID

You may not realize this, but your organization is haunted. I know this because every organization encounters the same sinister spirit that roams the halls looking for victims to oppress. I call this shifty shadow the *Narrative Void*.

The Narrative Void is a vacant space that occurs inside the organization when there's no story to keep everyone aligned. In extreme cases the Narrative Void can take up residence in the very center of the organization, splintering it into factions of disconnected efforts that never quite come together as a unified mission.

For years, companies have attempted to exorcise the Narrative Void using the most sacred document available: *the mission statement*. The corporate mission statement is like the holy grail of organizational effectiveness. With monastic dedication, executives gather for off-site retreats where they etch painstaking phrases onto tablets few will ever read and even fewer will understand or apply. Talk about a story going nowhere.

Needless to say, only in very rare cases has a mission *statement* actually led a company to be *on a mission*.

ARE YOUR PEOPLE CONFUSED?

The diagram below gives a snapshot of an organization infected with a Narrative Void. It paints a picture of many companies today. The different divisions across the organization exist in microcosms that can only be truly understood by the people who live in them. Left to themselves, these people must make decisions and develop strategies to meet demands. They assume these decisions only affect them. But along the way their choices create tiny overtones that ripple across the organization. From an organizational perspective, it's like bleeding to death from a thousand paper cuts.

As you can see, where there's no plot, there's no productivity.

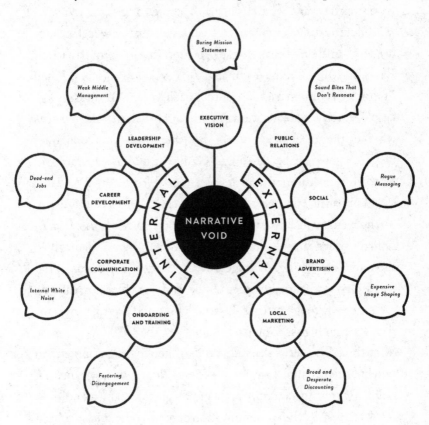

THE COST OF A NARRATIVE VOID

In the 1990s, Gallup began measuring the level of commitment employees felt toward their job and their employer. The numbers were startlingly low. Their research found that about one out of every five employees nationwide were truly excited about the work they were doing.[1] This is a problem. The obvious assumption is that an engaged associate gives more discretionary effort than someone who is not engaged. Not only that, but engaged associates took fewer sick days and were less likely to become a turnover statistic.

Gallup's discovery revealed that companies were losing hundreds of millions through gaps in productivity and efficiency. Back in 2012, Gallup estimated this was costing the United States $450 billion to $550 billion each year.[2] Needless to say, employers pay someone the same amount in salaries and benefits whether they're engaged or not. So when leaders of companies began to get their heads around Gallup's findings, the race was on to cure the disengagement epidemic.

As it turns out, one of the biggest contributors to the rise of disengagement has been the information explosion. As I mentioned earlier, people are bombarded with more than three thousand marketing messages every twenty-four hours. And that's just marketing messages. The number of non-marketing messages—through articles, Internet posts, and slanted news stories—is even higher. Compare that to, say, the 1970s. We've gone from three TV networks and one local newspaper to more than two hundred channels, millions of news blogs, podcasts, Internet radio, Twitter, Instagram, Facebook, Snapchat, and LinkedIn.

Meanwhile, the communication of most companies has been going in reverse. The personal interaction that once fueled connection in the workplace has been replaced by telecommuting, remote field offices, and conference calls. The days of catching up around the water cooler are gone. Granted, they've added e-mail blasts and an employee portal, but studies show readership of those outlets is minimal.

Could it be the white noise is a breeding ground for the Narrative Void? I don't think it's a coincidence.

A strong, StoryBrand-inspired narrative expels the Narrative

Void the way light drives out darkness. Companies who calibrate their activities around a common story don't just *state* their mission; they're *on a mission*. They didn't just dream about a better story, their culture tells one.

JUST BECAUSE YOU KNOW THE STORY DOESN'T MEAN YOUR TEAM DOES

So how does a StoryBrand BrandScript stop the bleeding? Let's look at how most workplaces work.

In many cases it starts with onboarding. Without a StoryBrand BrandScript, it usually goes like this: HR person welcomes new employee, issues a company key fob, and sits him down in front of a sexual harassment video for ten minutes. Next they skim through the company manual together and cover some light gossip about the personal life of a certain senior manager. A quick trip to the lobby to read the company mission statement, drop the new guy off at his cube, and the HR person is back at his desk in an hour. Done.

For the next three to five years, the new guy does a solid job meeting all the performance management metrics laid out by his supervisor. He earns three bonuses, one promotion, and the department's top award two years in a row—and never works past 6:00 p.m. He learns to navigate around the people who create resistance, picks his battles, accepts compromises, and absorbs occasional consequences. Then one afternoon a headhunter calls with a good-enough offer, and he's on to the next chapter of his life.

No boats were rocked. No stars were reached. For the company, there were wins and losses and a few ties. It's like a movie where nothing happens, nobody cares, and the popcorn's stale.

Is it any wonder the workplace is wracked by disengagement?

Did you notice the Narrative Void in this story? Without a unifying narrative at the center, there was nothing to inspire the new hire beyond the status quo. The company didn't do anything wrong. But they didn't do anything special either. In a competitive environment, that approach won't get you very far. That's the intoxicating deception of the Narrative Void. It lulls the company to sleep. And eventually to death.

GETTING THE ORGANIZATION BACK ON MISSION

When customers are invited into a magnificent story, it creates customer engagement. Could the same be true for employees? Absolutely.

With a StoryBrand-inspired narrative, ordinary jobs become extraordinary adventures. With a unifying BrandScript, the above story would have gone more like this:

Before even applying for a job, the prospective employee has already heard the buzz on the street about this cool company. It's somehow more alive. The people who work there love it and so do their customers. They exude a sense of competence within their industry as well as across the community in general. Their leaders are respected. Even their former employees talk about it with a hint of sentimental longing. On the list of ideal places to work, there are few that compare.

During the first interview, the candidate starts to understand where the buzz has been coming from. The hiring manager describes the company the way you might describe Lewis and

Clarke preparing to tame the western frontier. There are interesting characters whose lives have led them to this place. Business goals sound like plot twists. There are mountains to climb and rivers to cross. There are storms to weather, bears to hunt, and treasure to find. The hiring manager is visibly excited as she walks effortlessly through the seven categories of the company's narrative.

But not just anyone gets selected for this expedition. The employees of this company aren't trying to be snobs; they're just staying true to the story they're following and they don't want to compromise the plot. If you happen to be selected, it's because destiny basically demands it. Instantly the candidate's concept of work shifts up a level. It's no longer just about what he can get *out* of it. It's also about who he will become if he's allowed to enter the story. He senses that working for this company will transform him.

By the second and third interviews, the candidate has met most of the team and even been interviewed by them. Everyone he meets tells the exact same story he heard on the street and in the first interview. The story is growing on him. He realizes he *needs* to be part of a story like this to be fully satisfied in life. We all do.

Finally, his first day on the job arrives, and the onboarding experience is more like being adopted than getting hired. He spends quality time with a facilitator who takes a small, new team through a curriculum explaining the story of their customer and how the company positions themselves as the guide in their customers' story. Amazingly, the onboarding is more about the company's customers than it is about the company itself. This organization loves their customers and is obsessed with seeing them win the day. Finally, the new employee discovers the secret. These people are here to serve a customer they love.

Our new recruit is then invited to a special luncheon for

new hires hosted by the CEO. During the luncheon, the CEO delivers a short but powerful keynote based on the company's BrandScript. The keynote is invigorating, the CEO is intoxicating in his love for the company's customers, and the whole thing backs up what the new recruit learned during the onboarding course. The grand finale? A short film, based on the company's StoryBrand BrandScript, about the amazing impact the organization is making not only in business but also in the lives of individuals. Our new recruit asks the HR director if he can get a link to the video so he can send it to his friends and family, more or less bragging about his amazing new job.

For the next three to five years, the new guy feels like he's still getting to know the place. Every month he discovers new reasons why this is his dream job. Pictures of customers are plastered all over the walls, celebrating their successes. His daily tasks are not mundane but are specific objectives that have him working together with other teams to help their customers solve the problems that are frustrating them. His coworkers are not his competition but are a supportive community that actually wants him to thrive and grow as they live out a story about changing the world. Customers themselves visit the office to get a tour of the company that helped solve their problems.

Headhunters call every month with jobs that almost always represent a raise and a promotion. He usually forgets to call them back.

Across the organization, the people seem fully present not just physically but mentally. Productivity is high and efficiency is a matter of pride. Thanks to very low turnover, the organization maintains a rich repository of valuable experience that pays dividends most companies never realize.

Did you notice the alignment and consistency in this story? It's not because they gather around a plaque in the lobby each morning and sing the company song like a bunch of communists obeying a dictator's failed vision. If you didn't know their secret, you'd think everything just sort of fell into place spontaneously. But behind it all is a leadership team that understands the power of story, has created a StoryBrand BrandScript, and has learned to implement that narrative in every facet of the organization.

WHEN A MISSION COMES TO LIFE

Mission statements were never a bad idea. They were just never enough. In fact, a mission is exactly what people need in order to come together as a company. But a statement is inadequate to turn a mission into a story. It's like reading the tagline on a movie poster instead of seeing the actual movie.

Ben Ortlip is the director of the StoryBrand culture program. He specializes in implementing the StoryBrand Framework inside large organizations. A few years ago, a very popular fast-food restaurant chain approached his team about helping them with engagement. At the time, the brand had crossed the billion-dollar threshold and was experiencing about 5 percent growth. That might seem pretty solid to most people, but this place has amazing food and is made up of some of the finest people you'll meet. Ben felt like they should be doing better.

After spending some time at headquarters and behind the scenes in restaurants in several states, it was clear that some complacency had begun to set in. There was nothing wrong with their operations. The product was phenomenal. And their marketing was effective. The problem was they'd grown large enough, and in so many directions, they'd lost their plot. It's not unlike when a movie becomes a success and they turn it into a sequel. Often the story just feels forced.

IS YOUR *THOUGHTMOSPHERE* ON SCRIPT?

Killing off a Narrative Void isn't easy, and it takes time. Around the StoryBrand office, Ben uses the term *thoughtmosphere*. A thoughtmosphere is an invisible mixture of beliefs and ideas that drives employee behavior and performance. A thoughtmosphere improves when a StoryBrand-inspired narrative is created, talking points are devised, and a plan of execution is put in place to reinforce those talking points so every stakeholder understands their important role.

For the restaurant chain in question, this involved video curriculum, a series of regional meetings, a major national convention, and updates from the CEO often filmed in casual settings at headquarters. Retreats for franchise owners involved personal updates from the CEO followed by inspirational speakers who could speak into the organization's narrative. The company held concerts on the beach for just the stakeholders, and other brands who had a similar mission were discussed and publicly praised for their similar work serving customers.

Almost immediately you could sense a shift across the brand. There was renewed energy. People who hadn't been seen or heard from in years started showing up at meetings, ready to lock arms again. The Narrative Void was gone.

And tangible growth? In less than three years, the chain

went from 5 percent growth to nearly 30 percent, all with the very same people who had been inside the organization all along. For a billion-dollar company, that translated into hundreds of millions per year, every year.

The number one job of an executive is to remind the stakeholders what the mission is, over and over. And yet most executives can't really explain the overall narrative of the organization. Here's the problem: if an executive can't explain the story, team members will never know where or why they fit.

When your culture tells a great story, everybody wins. A company with a healthy culture looks something like this:

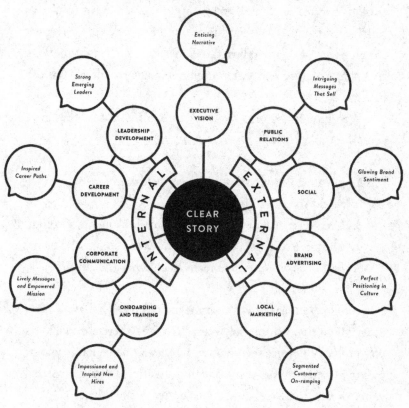

READY TO CHANGE YOUR COMPANY'S CULTURE?

A true mission isn't a *statement*; it's a way of living and being. A mission is more than token rituals that make momentary reference to the things your employees should care about. A mission is a story you reinforce through every department strategy, every operational detail, and every customer experience. That's what it means to be a company *on mission*.

And it all starts with your StoryBrand BrandScript.

We created the StoryBrand culture program to provide a turnkey service for larger organizations to achieve a full, custom implementation of their StoryBrand BrandScript—to weave the elements of their vital narrative into the important functions that shape culture and foster employee engagement around the mission.

We guide many organizations through a process that goes something like this:

1. Create a BrandScript with your leadership team.
2. Audit the existing *thoughtmosphere*.
3. Create a custom StoryBrand culture implementation plan.
4. Optimize internal communications to support the plan.
5. Install a self-sustained team to enhance the culture.

People often ask how a StoryBrand culture is different from everywhere else. I think they want a list. Yes, there are cool ideas you probably haven't seen before, like using behavioral typologies to identify job fit, or introducing a platform called a "virtual water cooler" to foster connections between coworkers.

The reality is most of the things StoryBrand culture does

look strangely similar to the things other companies do. It's just that StoryBrand cultures do these things while unified around a common, disciplined narrative.

A StoryBrand Culture Turns Their Entire Team into a Sales Force

The main distinction in a StoryBrand culture is their attention to how the basic blocking and tackling of business is synchronized around a StoryBrand BrandScript. The BrandScript filters out all the noise and lets each stakeholder, each day, know why they're doing what they're doing.

When team members understand the story of the organization and can explain it in short, disciplined sound-bites that have been reinforced through varying modes of communication from executives, they give words to potential customers that potential customers can use to spread the word. Brief, narrative ideas shared from inspired team members spread faster than muddled, confusing explanations shared by bored, disengaged employees.

A StoryBrand Culture Honors the Story of Its Team Members

When you leverage the StoryBrand Framework externally, for marketing, it transforms the *customer value proposition*. When you leverage it internally, for engagement, it transforms the *employee value proposition*.

All engagement rises and falls on the employee value proposition. Increasing compensation is one way you might add value to employees, but that's just the beginning. You can also raise value by improving the employee experience: advancement opportunities, recognition, meaningful work, camaraderie, and flexibility. All those things add value too.

To accomplish this, many StoryBrand BrandScripts are created. Certainly there is the external BrandScript that is pointed at the customer, but there are also BrandScripts created from the perspective of the leadership to the overall team. In these StoryBrand BrandScripts, the team is positioned as the hero and the company leadership is positioned as the guide. Compensation packages, leadership development, organized events, and more are all "tools" the leadership creates to help their employees win the day. Without understanding where a team member's narrative is going, compensation, development, and events are all fueling fires heading in a thousand directions.

We've found time and time again that leaders desire to be seen as heroes when, in actuality, everything they think they want from playing the hero only comes by playing the guide. Guides are respected, loved, listened to, understood, and followed loyally.

When the story of the customer and the story of the company align with the story of the team, we get an alchemy that is not only profitable, it's healing. Now that I've spent several years running a company that is on mission, I can never go back. There is more to life than dominating the market. Dominating the market is only a beautiful story if the team that accomplishes such a challenging task has tied that ambition to their own personal dreams.

Is your organization on a mission? Does every stakeholder you interact with understand the story of your customer and what role the organization plays in that story? And do they understand their personal role in this important narrative? If not, building your company around a compelling story may be the first step in a turnaround. Not just for the company, but for your customers, your team members, and even you.

Where there's no story, there's no engagement.

THE STORYBRAND MARKETING ROADMAP

Five (almost free) things you can
do to implement the StoryBrand
Framework and grow your business

So where do we go from here? Now that we have a StoryBrand BrandScript, how can we use these powerful messages so they have the greatest possible impact on our bottom line?

The StoryBrand Marketing Roadmap is your hassle-free "getting started" guide to implementing what you've accomplished in creating your BrandScript. If you've yet to create a BrandScript, either attend one of our workshops live or online, or go back and follow the process outlined in this book.

Once your StoryBrand BrandScript is created, you'll likely want to refine your website. We consider this the first and most important step you can take to grow your business, and that's why we separated that step into a previous chapter. Not only will editing your website grow your business, but it will help you and your team understand the basic talking points of your new and improved message.

Once your website has been edited so that it communicates clearly, we consider this roadmap the most effective next step most businesses can take to see an impact.

Of the thousands of clients we've worked with, these five marketing and messaging efforts (along with editing their website so it works) get the best results regardless of whether our clients are running a small business or a multibillion-dollar company. And the great news is, they're nearly free. I mean, they're going to cost you some time, but you won't have to hire a giant advertising firm to see results.

What are the five (almost free) things you can do to grow your business?

Here they are:

1. **Create a One-liner.** This roadmap is going to teach you the four-part formula for creating a single statement that will grow your business. You'll want to memorize this statement yourself and repeat it any time somebody asks you what you do. You can teach your one-liner to your staff and feature it on your website, in e-mail signatures, and even on the back of your business card. People are wondering how you can make their lives better, and we're going to show you how to tell them in such a way that they will want to engage with your brand.

2. **Create a Lead Generator and Collect E-mail Addresses.** You need a lead generator. You need a PDF, e-course,

video series, webinar, live event, or just about anything else that will allow you to collect e-mail addresses. A lead generator will help you find qualified buyers so you can let them know, directly and authoritatively, how you can help them resolve their problems. This may be the single most important piece of collateral you create in response to this book, and in this roadmap, I'll show you how.

3. **Create an Automated E-Mail Drip Campaign.** Marketing has changed, and even the largest of companies are diversifying their ad spend to include e-mail campaigns. But where is the best place to get started? By far, you'll get your best results through an automated drip campaign. In this section, I'll give you the basics. Once you start collecting e-mail addresses and using a beginner's nurturing campaign, it will be as though you've employed a sales team that works for you while you sleep.

4. **Collect and Tell Stories of Transformation.** Almost every story is about the transformation of the hero, and when we tell stories about how we've helped our customers transform, potential customers immediately understand what your brand can offer them. In this section, I'll help you collect stories of transformation, teaching you what questions to specifically ask your customers and where to use those stories to get the greatest response from potential customers.

5. **Create a System That Generates Referrals.** Once you create a system that funnels potential customers into becoming actual customers, your work is not quite done. The final step is to turn around and invite happy customers to become evangelists for your brand. This will only happen

if we create a system that invites and incentivizes them to spread the word. The StoryBrand Marketing Roadmap will close out with a step-by-step guide, as well as outside-the-box ideas, for incentivizing your existing customers to tell their friends about your products and services.

YOUR STEP-BY-STEP PLAN

Each step of the StoryBrand Marketing Roadmap will help your company in percentages. The more you execute, the clearer your message will become and the more your company will grow.

The roadmap may take you a few months or even a year to execute, but don't worry. You should see results with each step.

If you'd like to hire a Certified StoryBrand Guide to take you through the roadmap, you can search for the guide who is right for you at www.clarifyyourmessage.com. Certified StoryBrand Guides are independent contractors who act as marketing coaches and consultants and are each certified through an immersive, live training program. They are specifically trained to help you clarify your message and execute this roadmap to get the greatest result.

Whether you hire a guide or go it alone, these are five of the most successful ways our clients have implemented their new and improved message. Consider this roadmap to be a checklist. Once you've created a StoryBrand BrandScript using the SB7 Framework, refined your website so it is clear and compelling, and executed each of the five tasks on the StoryBrand Marketing Roadmap, you will save money and grow your company.

STORYBRAND ROADMAP TASK ONE: CREATE A ONE-LINER FOR YOUR COMPANY

Most business leaders lose the sale the second they start talking about their business. When somebody asks what we do and we answer by rolling our eyes and saying, "Well, it's complicated" or "Well, my grandfather started the company . . ." we've lost the customer's interest immediately. Instead, imagine memorizing a single statement you could repeat after anybody asks what you do. And imagine that statement being relevant to the needs of potential customers. Imagine this statement being so powerful it causes people to ask for your business card.

A one-liner is a new and improved way to answer the question "What do you do?" It's more than a slogan or tagline; it's a single statement that helps people realize why they need your products or services.

To understand how it works, let's take another page out of the Hollywood playbook. When writers pitch their screenplays to studio executives, the difference between being accepted or rejected often comes down to what's called a *logline*.

A logline is simply a movie's one-sentence description. A strong logline sells the screenplay and continues to be used all the way through a movie's opening weekend. If you've ever scrolled through a movie app on your phone or on Netflix looking for something to watch, chances are you've read a logline. Here are a few examples:

"A precocious private high school student whose life revolves around his school competes with its most famous and successful alumnus for the affection of a first-grade teacher."—*Rushmore*

"Blacksmith Will Turner teams up with eccentric pirate 'Captain' Jack Sparrow to save his love, the governor's daughter, from Jack's former pirate allies, who are now undead."—*Pirates of the Caribbean: The Curse of the Black Pearl*

"A science-fiction fantasy about a naive but ambitious farm boy from a backwater desert who discovers powers he never knew he had when he teams up with a feisty princess, a mercenary space pilot, and an old wizard warrior to lead a ragtag rebellion against the sinister forces of the evil Galactic Empire."—*Star Wars: A New Hope*

"An incompetent, immature, and dimwitted heir to an auto-parts factory must save the business to keep it out of the hands of his new con-artist relatives and big business."—*Tommy Boy*

What makes these loglines complete and effective? Two things: imagination and intrigue. They summarize the movie in a way that a viewer can imagine the story, and they do so with enough intrigue that they make the reader want to watch the film.

The one-liner you will create for your company will work like a logline in a movie; it will intrigue qualified buyers and invite them to do business with you.

Now imagine everybody in your company memorizing your one-liner. What would life look like if everybody you worked with were converted into a sales force spreading the word about your products and services? Creating a one-liner and repeating it over and over is a great way to spread the word about what you do.

To craft a compelling one-liner, we'll employ a distilled version of the StoryBrand Framework. If you use the following four components, you'll craft a powerful one-liner:

1. THE CHARACTER
2. THE PROBLEM
3. THE PLAN
4. THE SUCCESS

Your one-liner doesn't have to be a single sentence, nor does it need to be four sentences. Think of it more as a statement. You simply want to communicate these four ideas. Who is your customer? What is their problem? What is your plan to help them, and what will their life look like after you do?

Let's take a deeper look at each of the four necessary components:

1. THE CHARACTER

If you've created a StoryBrand BrandScript, you've done the heavy lifting when it comes to understanding who your character is and what they want. Let's say your demographic is soccer moms and you sell a Pilates class. Your one-liner might be, "We help busy mothers get a weekly, meaningful workout so they feel healthy and full of energy." If you sell vacation rentals to retired couples you might say, "We save retirees the cost of a second home in Florida, yet deliver the warm beaches and luxury accommodations they love." These examples start with a character. A busy mom. A retiree. People need to be able to say "That's me!" when they hear your one-liner.

2. THE PROBLEM

As I said earlier in the book, stories hinge on conflict, so we should never shy away from talking about our customers' challenges. Defining a problem triggers the thought in your customer's mind: *Yeah, I do struggle with that. Will your brand be able to help me overcome it?*

Soccer moms are challenged with busy schedules, and they can never seem to find time to work out. A retired couple looking to spend their winter in Florida cringes at the cost of buying a second home. But defining the problem is vital, because once you do you've opened a story loop and they'll be looking to you to help them find a resolution.

3. THE PLAN

You won't be able to spell out your entire plan in your one-liner, but you must hint at it. For workout-deprived soccer moms, the plan might be weekly, meaningful workouts. For the retired couple, the plan of a time-share can make the difference.

When a customer reads your one-liner, the plan component should cause them to think, *Well, when it's organized that way, it makes sense. Perhaps there's hope.*

4. THE SUCCESS

This is where you paint a picture of what life could look like after customers use your product or service. For soccer moms, success may involve a sense of health, well-being, or attractiveness. For retired couples looking for a second home in Florida, success could be as simple as warm, enjoyable winters.

Let's put it all together by crafting a one-liner for soccer moms to see how powerful a one-liner actually is.

- The Character: Moms
- The Problem: Busy schedules

- The Plan: Short, meaningful workouts
- The Success: Health and renewed energy
- "We provide busy moms with a short, meaningful workout they can use to stay healthy and have renewed energy."

Contrast that statement with the description most business leaders might give: "I run a gym."

If you're a busy soccer mom, your ears would perk up because the new one-liner identifies you, helps you overcome your problem, gives you a plan, and promises a better life. A statement like this will invite customers into a better story they can actually live.

What about our retired couple?

- The Character: Retired couples
- The Problem: A second mortgage
- The Plan: A time-share option
- The Success: Avoiding those cold, northern winters
- "We help retired couples who want to escape the harsh cold avoid the hassle of a second mortgage while still enjoying the warm, beautiful weather of Florida in the winter."

Again, compare this statement to what most business leaders would say: "Well, it's complicated. I got involved in real estate several years ago and then when we had our second kid we moved to Florida . . ." Boring. Noise.

At StoryBrand, our one-liner is "Most business leaders don't know how to talk about their company, so we created a framework that helps them simplify their message, create great marketing material, connect with customers, and grow their business." Again, a one-liner is simply a clear, repeatable statement that allows potential customers to find themselves in the story a company is telling.

Keep Editing Your One-Liner Until It Works

Consider your first one-liner a rough draft. Write it down and test it repeatedly. Run it by your friends, spouse, potential customers, even strangers standing in line at Starbucks. Do people look interested? Do they completely understand what you offer? If so, you're on the right track. When they start asking for your business card or for more information, you've really dialed it in.

How to Use Your One-Liner

Once you've created your one-liner, use it liberally. Here are a few ways to put it to work:

1. **Memorize your one-liner and repeat it over and over.** There's a good chance you've become so used to rambling about your business that reciting your one-liner won't come naturally. Memorize it as though you're an actor in a movie and it's your most important line. Read and repeat it until you can recite it as fast as your own name. This will take some time, but it might be the best few hours you spend working on your new messaging campaign.

2. **Have your team memorize the one-liner.** Now it's time to get your team to own the one-liner. That includes everyone from the CEO to the guy who mows the lawn. If every team member can repeat the one-liner, you will have converted your staff into a viral sales force. Have

fun with this! Print the one-liner on your walls, coffee cups, T-shirts, or anything else your team interacts with daily. After each member of your team memorizes the one-liner, they will be spreading a clear and compelling message about your company at every cocktail party and baseball game they attend.

Be prepared, though, because you'll be amazed at how hard this really is. Branding is difficult and it will take time. Carry around a wad of five-dollar bills and ask somebody in the office each day what your company does. If someone answers with the one-liner, reward him or her with a crisp five. Soon, word will spread around the office and people will know they need to get this down. It might cost you a thousand dollars by the time you're done, but I assure you, it will be the best money you've spent marketing your company.

3. **Include it on your website.** While it's largely subjective what words you include on your website, make sure to get your one-liner in there somewhere. Even a small paragraph beneath the main section of your website will do. Including your one-liner almost guarantees your site invites potential customers into a story they find interesting. Make it bold and legible so it becomes one of the obvious statements you want viewers to read.

4. **Repeat your one-liner in every piece of marketing collateral possible.** Use your one-liner till it feels borderline excessive. Include your one-liner in every piece of marketing possible. Our customers aren't going to read every one of our e-mails or visit our webpage every day. The more opportunities a customer has to read or hear our

one-liner, the more likely they will be to understand how we can make their lives better.

Print your one-liner on your business cards and in your social media bios. Print it on your packaging. Include it in your e-mail signature. Repeat it over and over to increase the percentage chance customers will read it.

I recently attended a benefit concert in which a bunch of A-list musicians passed a guitar around to raise money for a nonprofit. Even though these artists had written hundreds of songs among them, I noticed they only played their hits. Had this been their own show, they would have played lesser-known songs or mixed in new ones, but since they could each only play a few songs, they played the crowd's favorites.

Have you ever considered what it's like to be a big-time music star? The adoring crowds and star treatment are great, but life on stage can get rather repetitive. I've often wondered how difficult it must be for James Taylor to sing "Fire and Rain" again and again, night after night, decade after decade. What's worse is he can never mail it in—each night the crowds are different, and he has to deliver a song first released in 1970 with fresh energy and passion every time.

That's the discipline it takes to be successful. James Taylor sings the same song over and over again because ultimately he's a servant of the people. He's a brilliant artist, but he's also a professional, and professionals do what it takes to please their customers, pay the bills, and grow their brand.

When you think about how often you'll need to say your one-liner, think of yourself as a big music star. Amateurs ramble on, playing and saying whatever they want, but professionals serve their audience. Our one-liner is like our hit song, and we need to say it over and over and over until even our customers have it memorized and start repeating it to their friends.

ROADMAP TASK TWO: CREATE A LEAD-GENERATOR AND COLLECT E-MAIL ADDRESSES

Quick question: What is the most sacred, private, personal possession you own today? The one thing you'd be terrified of other people having full, unmitigated access to?

I'm going to take a wild guess and say it's your smartphone.

If you think about it, there's an awful lot of your life—photos, texts, and apps—stored up in that little device. It's also very likely there's one important account on your phone that acts as a gateway to nearly every other component of your life:

Your e-mail account.

If this is true of you, it's also true of your customers. An e-mail account is one of the most sacred, personal things people possess. But what if you could have a direct line to customers through that very channel? What if customers willingly gave you permission to contact them in such a personal way?

That's e-mail marketing. E-mail is the most valuable and effective way you can spread the word about your business, especially if your company revenue is under $5 million and you don't have a large marketing budget. As of this writing I have hundreds of thousands of Twitter followers and nearly as many Facebook fans, but all my social media platforms combined don't perform anywhere close to sending out an update or offer via e-mail.

Busting the Myth of the Newsletter Signup

Most business leaders who come to one of our workshops think e-mail doesn't work because so few people sign up for their newsletter. I hate to be the bearer of bad news, but no one wants to sign up for your newsletter. Nobody wants to sign up to "stay in the loop," because this kind of offer doesn't promise anything of value. The only thing it implies is spam.

So how do we get people to join our e-mail list? We offer them something valuable in return, something more valuable than the vague offer of a newsletter. This "something" is a lead generator, a resource that magnetically attracts people to our businesses and invites them to take action. In the StoryBrand Framework, we call this a *transitional call to action*. A transitional call to action, if you remember, is like asking potential customers out on a date. We're not asking them to commit, but we are asking them to spend a little more time with us.

How to Create an Irresistible Lead Generator

In order to combat noise in today's marketplace, your lead generator must do two things:

1. Provide enormous value for your customer
2. Establish you as an authority in your field

In the year we started StoryBrand, our first lead generator was a simple, downloadable document (in PDF format) called "5 Things Your Website Should Include." It was remarkably successful. More than forty thousand people downloaded it, which allowed me to e-mail reminders about our upcoming StoryBrand Marketing Workshops. I credit that single lead generator with taking our company past the $2 million mark. From there, we created a free video series called The 5-Minute Marketing Makeover (http://fiveminutemarketingmakeover. com), which took our lead generation to another level. We were no longer grinding to create business. Now we create lead generators for each revenue stream our company offers. This allows us to segment our customers by their interests and offer different products to solve their various problems.

There are endless options for creating lead generators. Our clients have been incredibly creative in offering valuable information and services in exchange for an e-mail address. Of all we've created and we've seen our clients create, there are five that are most effective.

Five Types of Lead Generators for All Types of Businesses

1. **Downloadable Guide:** This is a shockingly inexpensive way to generate leads, and it's what we used when launching StoryBrand. Get specific. If you're a local market selling produce, offer monthly recipes or tips for tending a garden.

2. **Online Course or Webinar:** Creating a brief online course or webinar is involved, but it's also easier than ever. If you're an expert on something and want to position yourself as such in the marketplace, offer a free training online in exchange for an e-mail address. By doing so, you'll have positioned yourself as an expert, created reciprocity, and earned your customer's trust.

3. **Software Demos or a Free Trial:** This has worked wonders for many businesses. Remember in the early nineties when AOL sent demo CDs in the mail with one thousand

hours of free Internet browsing for forty-five days? They worked like a charm. The Internet has changed since then, but the marketing principle remains the same.

4. **Free Samples:** My wife, Betsy, orders ready-to-cook meals from a business called Blue Apron. To generate more leads, Blue Apron credits her with "free sample meals" she can send to friends and family. A number of them try it, and they end up buyers.

5. **Live Events:** If you've ever walked into a large pet store like Petco, you've likely seen invitations to free dog obedience classes. Even if you're a smaller operation, hosting a quarterly class is a terrific way to build a small database of qualified customers.

Still Stuck? Swipe Ideas from These Examples

One key to having an effective lead generator is to give it an irresistible title. These are some sample lead generators I've seen that worked well. There's no need to reinvent the wheel. Leverage these proven examples and create something similar.

"5 Mistakes People Make with Their First Million Dollars"—A downloadable PDF guide offered by a financial advisor who wanted to find young, newly wealthy clients to help them with their financial planning.

"Building Your Dream Home: 10 Things to Get Right Before You Build"—A free e-book offered by an architect who wanted to establish herself as a guide to families looking to build a custom home.

"Cocktail Club: Learn to Make One New Cocktail Each Month"—This was a monthly event surprisingly put on by a garden store that taught attendees how to infuse bitters and simple syrups with herbs. The objective for this promotion was to create a community around their store. Business is booming (or should I say blooming) because people want to attend their classes.

"Becoming a Professional Speaker"—A free online course offered by a speaking coach for those who wanted to become professional speakers. This generated leads for long-term subscriptions to his coaching service.

The ideas go on and on. Now that you're aware of lead generators, you'll see them everywhere. Keep a running list of lead generator possibilities. If one strikes you as abnormally strong, get to work and create a version of your own. The key here is to avoid falling into "paralysis by analysis." The best and easiest place to start is with a downloadable guide in PDF format. If you aren't a writer, don't worry. There are plenty of writers for hire, and you can find some terrific StoryBrand Certified Copywriters through our directory at clarifyyourmessage.com.

The process is quite simple: Have the writer interview you about your area of expertise, and he or she will flesh out the content. You can then send the final draft to a designer to lay out. The process is fast and inexpensive and will yield tremendous results.

How Much Value Should I Give Away for Free?

This is one of the most common questions we get asked. My response: be as generous as possible. To my knowledge, it's never cost me to give away valuable, free content. People consume this content on the run and will gladly pay to attend a workshop or hire a facilitator that helps them slow down and learn the information at a custom-created pace.

If you're going to create a downloadable PDF, keep it to about three pages of content. Stuff as much value as you can into those three pages so your prospects will see you as the "go-to" guide.

Among marketers, it's been said you give away the "why"—as in why a potential customer would need to address or be aware of a certain issue—and sell the "how," which is where you offer a tool or teach customers how to follow through step-by-step. My personal belief is that we should be generous—very generous. At StoryBrand, we certainly give away the "why," but we also give away an awful lot of the "how." It's never cost me to be generous with my customers.

How Many E-mail Addresses Do We Need to Get Started?

This is a common question, and I'm going to give the common answer: it depends. A financial advisor may get "above the grind" with five hundred e-mail addresses, but those may take years to acquire. A national or global business may need hundreds of thousands of e-mails that are further segmented based on demographic information. But if your business is generating less than $5 million a year, you should see results with as little as two hundred and fifty qualified e-mail addresses.

Where Should I Feature My Lead Generator?

Make sure you feature your lead generator liberally on your website. I recommend creating a pop-up feature on your site that, after ten seconds or so of the browser arriving, offers your resource to the user. Though people complain about pop-ups, the stats are clear: they readily outperform nearly every other type of Internet advertising. Just make sure there's a ten-second buffer. You don't want the pop-up to appear immediately. That would be like being tackled by a salesman as soon as you walk through the door of a retail store.

Like farming a field, building a healthy and engaged e-mail list takes time, but it's time well spent. Start today. A year from now, you'll be glad you did.

ROADMAP TASK THREE: CREATE AN AUTOMATED E-MAIL DRIP CAMPAIGN

In my midtwenties, after having spent a year or more traveling around the country in a Volkswagen van, I got a warehouse job at a publishing company outside Portland, Oregon. The job came to me by accident. A friend's dad owned the company and noticed I needed a job. But I'm grateful. Working in publishing, even in an entry-level position, helped me fall in love with books.

Within a few years of getting that job, I was put in charge of the company. It was an unintentional move on the owner's part because people kept retiring or taking other jobs and the owner kept "temporarily" moving me up. One season, though, the owner hired a consultant to help him figure out what to do, and after studying the numbers, the consultant pointed at me and said, "Put that guy on commission and let him do what he wants." I was just as taken aback as my boss. Without any of us realizing it, the company had actually started growing. And when we sat down and looked closely at the numbers, we realized the reason.

Just before my series of promotions, I'd discovered a piece of software called FileMaker Pro. We used this software to manage our database and orders. I passed the hours fiddling around with the software and one day realized we could see who had placed the largest orders each month and send them a letter in the mail. This is all standard marketing these days, but back then it was relatively new technology. Each month I sent about two hundred form letters to the businesses that ordered the most copies of our books. That simple activity generated a ton of business.

The letters I wrote to our customers contained anything but good sales copy. One of the letters was about a camping trip I'd taken as a kid! Shakespearean plots, these were not.

These days my letters get a lot bigger response, but looking back, even those terrible letters worked to grow our business. And yet all our customers were doing was taking them from a pile of mail on their desk and throwing them away.

So why did the company grow if people weren't even reading my letters?

What I realized, in hindsight, was that every month our top customers were being reminded that we existed. Every time one of those customers threw a letter away, even without opening it, our logo was flashing across their eyes.

Content is important, but the point is, there is great power in simply reminding our customers we exist. I was young and dumb at the time, but I'd stumbled onto something. Our customers may not need our product today, and they might not need it tomorrow, but on the day they do need it, we want to make sure they remember who we are, what we have, and where they can reach us.

Send Potential Customers Regular, Valuable E-mails

The days of direct mail aren't completely dead, but it goes without saying that e-mail has largely taken over. Now that you've obtained e-mail addresses through your lead generator, the next step is to create an automated e-mail campaign.

An automated e-mail campaign is a terrific way to remind customers that you exist. And if they happen to open your e-mail (you'll be surprised at how many people actually do), then it's a great way to invite them into the story you're telling as a company.

An automated e-mail campaign is a prewritten sequence of e-mail messages that trigger once a person is added to your list. Some people call this an "auto-responder series" or a "funnel," but the idea is that you'll be inviting people into a narrative that leads to a sale even while you sleep.

Does Anybody Read These Things?

Don't worry if the open rates on these e-mails are low. A 20 percent open rate is industry standard, so anything above that is performing well. And remember, even if a person sees and deletes an e-mail, the goal has been accomplished: you are "branding" yourself into their universe.

If someone unsubscribes from your list, that's a good thing. That person will probably never buy from you anyway, and it reduces the size of your list so you aren't paying your e-mail service provider for e-mails that are dead weight. The last thing you want to do in your marketing is bother someone, so if someone unsubscribes, all the better. It's more important to have a list of qualified, interested subscribers than a large number of people who never intend to buy.

I subscribe to plenty of mailing lists that I hardly open an e-mail from. Why don't I unsubscribe? Because every twenty or so e-mails, they send something I actually want to open. Yet all those e-mails I delete are further branding those companies into my consciousness.

Getting Started

While there are many kinds of automated e-mail campaigns, the one we recommend starting with is the *nurturing campaign*. A nurturing campaign is a simple, regular e-mail that offers your subscribers valuable information as it relates to your products or services.

Not unlike our lead generator, we want these e-mails to continue positioning us as the guide and to create a bond of trust and reciprocity with potential customers. There will come a time to ask for a sale, but this isn't the primary goal of a nurturing campaign. A typical nurturing campaign may have an e-mail going out once each week, and the order might look like this:

E-mail #1: Nurturing e-mail
E-mail #2: Nurturing e-mail
E-mail #3: Nurturing e-mail
E-mail #4: Sales e-mail with a call to action

This pattern can be repeated month after month. I recommend creating a few months' worth of material and letting it ride, then adding to it as you have time. The idea is to offer something of great value and then occasionally ask for an order and remind people you have products and services that can make their lives better. Pretty soon you'll have hundreds of potential customers being introduced to your business. When they need help in your area of expertise, they will remember you and place an order.

So what's the difference between a nurturing e-mail and an e-mail with an offer and call to action?

The Nurturing E-mail

A good way to craft each nurturing e-mail is to use an effective formula that offers simple, helpful advice to a customer. I've been using this formula for years and customers love it.

1. Talk about a problem.
2. Explain a plan to solve the problem.
3. Describe how life can look for the reader once the problem is solved.

I also recommend including a postscript, or the P.S. Often, the P.S. is the only thing somebody who opens a mass e-mail will actually read.

That's really it. If you cover these three areas as efficiently as possible, you'll be crafting e-mails your customers open, read, and remember.

A GOOD NURTURING E-MAIL

Recently we consulted with the owner of a dog boarding company interested in growing her business. We recommended she create a lead-generating PDF called "5 Things Your Dog

Thinks About When You're Away" in exchange for the e-mail addresses of qualified customers. What dog lover wouldn't want to read a PDF with a title like that? Perfect.

A few days after somebody downloaded the PDF, they would get the first e-mail in the nurturing campaign. It looked like this:

Subject: Should We Free Feed Our Dogs?

Dear Name,

At Crest Hill Boarding we're often asked whether it's okay to free feed our dogs. It's certainly the easiest way to make sure a dog always has food and never goes hungry. But there are some problems with free feeding. Dogs that are free fed often gain excess fat later in life and health problems can occur without our noticing.

We recommend feeding your dog a set amount, once or twice per day. After twenty minutes, if your pet hasn't eaten their food, we recommend discarding the excess and waiting until the next set time to feed them again.

By sticking to a set amount and set schedule, you'll be able to monitor what your dog eats and also be able to diagnose any illness your pet may be suffering from that is making them lose their appetite. This will ensure your dog stays healthy and happy long into their life.

Here's to enjoying our pets for a long, long time.

Sincerely,

X

P.S. As for how much each dog should be fed, it really depends on how old your dog is and how big. Next time you and your dog are in the shop, introduce us to your dog and we'll tell you everything we know about the breed.

The bottom of this e-mail contained our client's logo, their one-liner, and a phone number in case anyone was ready to place an order. Still, getting an order wasn't the primary concern. The primary concern was to offer something of value, position the business as the guide, and create reciprocity.

You can see how getting a weekly e-mail like this would make our client's kennel stand out in any dog owner's mind. The next time a potential customer had to suddenly leave town, they'd fondly remember her kennel and take their dog in for boarding.

After three more e-mails like this, our client included an e-mail that contained an offer and a call to action.

The Offer and Call to Action E-mail

About every third or fourth e-mail in a nurturing campaign should offer a product or service to the customer. The key here is to be direct. You don't want to be passive, because being passive communicates weakness. In this e-mail you are clearly making an offer.

The formula might look like this:

1. Talk about a problem.
2. Describe a product you offer that solves this problem.
3. Describe what life can look like for the reader once the problem is solved.
4. Call the customer to a direct action leading to a sale.

A GOOD OFFER AND CALL TO ACTION E-MAIL

Similar to the nurturing e-mail, the offer and call-to-action e-mail aims to solve a problem. The only difference is that the solution is your product and a strong call to action has been inserted. You are inviting this subscriber to do business with you. Here's an offer and call-to-action e-mail we wrote for Crest Hill dog kennel:

Subject: A solution for scary boarding

Dear Name,

If you're anything like us, you hate leaving your dog behind when you go out of town. And you hate the idea of your dog being locked in a crate next to a bunch of other stress-inducing, barking dogs. As dog lovers, we used to hate that feeling too, and that's why we created Crest Hill Boarding.

At Crest Hill, your dog plays so hard all day, they are eager to lie down at night. We have three full-time staff members throwing tennis balls and enticing dogs to run and play so they're far too distracted to realize they're anywhere other than a second home. This means that by the end of the day all the other dogs are eager to sleep too, and so your dog rests comfortably. You won't believe how quiet our kennels are once we put the dogs to bed at 8 p.m.

Right now you can book three nights at Crest Hill at half price. This is a one-time offer and it's meant to introduce you to how differently we take care of your pet. We think once you see how eager your dog will be to join us, you'll feel better when you have to leave town. No more guilt. No more sad good-byes.

To take advantage of this offer, just call us. You don't even have to know when the next time you're going to leave town is, we will just mark you in our system as having taken advantage of the offer.

Call us today at 555-5555.

We can't wait for your dog to experience the Crest Hill difference.

Sincerely,

X

P.S. Make sure to call today. The call will only take a couple of minutes, and you'll be in our system forever. After you call, your dog's favorite home away from home will be waiting whenever you're in need of a safe, reliable, and fun-for-your dog solution.

This e-mail weaves in a tremendous amount of content from Crest Hill's StoryBrand BrandScript, including the external problem and internal fear of the customer along with elements from the success module. But the gist of the e-mail is that if a subscriber purchases Crest Hill's offer, one of their concerns will be resolved.

Note that the call to action is strong and contains a degree of scarcity because it is a one-time offer. Anyone who reads this e-mail knows exactly what we want them to do: board their dog at Crest Hill.

What Software Should We Use?

There are many software options when it comes to creating an automated e-mail campaign. If you're working with a designer or advertising agency, this is likely a question for them. You want your designer to work with whatever software they're accustomed to using.

If you want to create the system yourself, MailChimp is a fantastic service, especially for automated e-mail campaigns that are simple and reliable.

If you have a robust list and want to segment your audience, provide e-commerce solutions, take advantage of advanced strategies, and create a powerful e-mail force to be reckoned with, we recommend Infusionsoft. At StoryBrand we use Infusionsoft with great success. Our friends at Infusionsoft are working on template e-mails developed in coordination with the StoryBrand team to ensure e-mails that get a response. You can learn more about these e-mail templates at storybrand.com/infusionsoft.

Start Small

Getting an e-mail campaign up and running can be intimidating, but it doesn't have to be. Make sure to start small. To get started, simply open a Word document and start writing your e-mails. You can paste your e-mails into an e-mail application later. Writing that initial e-mail is the first step. Once you read it back to yourself, you're going to want to send it to customers. That's the beginning. Before you know it, you'll have a robust system of e-mails that are engaging customers at all hours of the day, even while you sleep.

ROADMAP TASK FOUR: COLLECT AND TELL STORIES OF TRANSFORMATION

As we learned earlier in the book, few things are more foundational to a compelling story than the transformation of the hero. Why? Because transformation is a core desire for every human being. That's why so many stories are about the hero being transformed into somebody better.

People love movies about characters who transform, and they love businesses that help them experience transformation themselves. One of the best ways we can illustrate how we help our customers transform is through customer testimonials.

Great testimonials give future customers the gift of going second. The challenge lies in getting the right kind of testimonial: one that showcases your value, the results you get for customers, and the experience people had working with you. Simply asking for a testimonial usually won't work because customers will share their feelings about you by default. "Nancy is a great friend! We highly recommend Nancy and her team!"

While those are nice words, they do very little in telling a story of transformation. There are no specific results mentioned or details about what life is like now that the transformation has taken place.

If you're asking customers to write a testimonial for you, it's likely they are (1) too busy to give deep thought to writing the testimonial or (2) subpar writers or communicators.

Weaving together a compelling tale of transformation means you have to ask the right questions—you need some raw materials to work with. The following questions will allow you to build a bank of compelling testimonials that work with nearly any customer quickly and easily.

These questions work because they "lead" the client down a specific train of thought. Simply use these questions to create a form customers can fill out. Once they fill out the form, the natural flow of the sentences will allow you to copy and paste the answers to build a client case study.

These same questions can also be used to create video testimonials. Simply invite customers to be interviewed and ask them the following questions. Once the video is edited and b-roll is inserted, you can feature your video on your website or in a nurturing or sales e-mail campaign.

Here are five questions most likely to generate the best response for a customer testimonial:

1. What was the problem you were having before you discovered our product?
2. What did the frustration feel like as you tried to solve that problem?
3. What was different about our product?
4. Take us to the moment when you realized our product was actually working to solve your problem.
5. Tell us what life looks like now that your problem is solved or being solved.

You can see the arc of the questions naturally yields a transformation story. Once you capture the testimonial, feature it everywhere: e-mails, promo videos, keynote speeches, live interviews, events. One season we closed each episode of the *Building a StoryBrand* podcast with an interview with someone who transformed their business and their life by applying the StoryBrand Framework. The response was overwhelming. We noted an immediate uptick in registrations for our marketing workshops.

The point is that people are drawn to transformation. When they see transformation in others, they want it for themselves. The more we feature the transformation journey our customers have experienced, the faster our business will grow.

ROADMAP TASK FIVE: CREATE A SYSTEM THAT GENERATES REFERRALS

Ask any business owner how they get new customers and the majority will say "word of mouth." It would seem obvious, then, that every business out there has a system for generating more word-of-mouth referrals. Unfortunately, that's seldom the case.

Once you create a system that funnels potential customers into becoming actual customers, the final step is to turn around and invite happy customers to become evangelists for your brand. This will only happen if you create a system that invites and incentivizes people to spread the word. Various studies conducted by the American Marketing Association have shown that referrals and peer recommendations are up to 2.5 times more responsive than any other marketing channel.

If you've done the simple, fun work of creating your StoryBrand BrandScript, your message should be clear. Now it's time to implement a system that gets people repeating that message to their friends and family.

Let's take a step-by-step look at what it takes to create an effective referral system.

1. IDENTIFY YOUR EXISTING, IDEAL CUSTOMERS

At the top of the current Domino's Pizza website there's a link that says, "Don't have a pizza profile? Create one." That link, even though it's in small print, is a huge moneymaker. Those who frequently order from the restaurant chain use this link to build their perfect pizza and enter their credit card information to order it. Domino's then sends them occasional prompts to reorder, especially before big events like important football games or holiday weekends when they know their customers are likely to enjoy their product.

Now imagine taking that strategy to the next level. What if creating a special database of existing, passionate customers and communicating with them differently can help you generate referrals? Developing a simple campaign using tools your existing fans can use to spread the word about your brand is key. Not only could you increase your existing business, but these happy customers will become an activated sales force and invite their friends.

2. GIVE YOUR CUSTOMERS A REASON TO SPREAD THE WORD

A few years ago, I utilized the services of a consulting firm that, as part of their system, asked me for a list of referrals. The request made me immediately uncomfortable. I felt like they wanted to use me for my friends, or worse, turn me into one of their salespeople.

That said, the service they provided was good, and had they framed the request another way, I might have complied. Specifically, it would have been nice if they'd have created a small, educational video that would have been valuable to my friends. I'd much more quickly pass along a video than I would hand over my friends' e-mail addresses.

Consider creating a PDF or video that you automatically send to existing clients along with an e-mail that goes something like this:

Dear Friend,

Thanks for doing business with us. A number of our clients have wanted to tell their friends about how we help customers, but they aren't sure how to do so. We've put together a little video that will help your friends solve *X problem*. If you have any friends with *X problem*, feel free to send it along. We'd be happy to follow up with any of them, and we'll be sure to let you know whether we could help.

We know you value your relationships and so do we. If your friends are experiencing a problem we've helped you solve, we'd love to help them too. If there's anything else we can do, please let us know.

Sincerely,
Nancy

P.S. X Problem can be frustrating. If you'd rather introduce us to your friend in person, just let us know. We are more than happy to meet with them in their place of business or at our office.

3. OFFER A REWARD

If you really want to prime the pump, offer a reward to existing clients who refer their friends. As I mentioned earlier, my wife has invited dozens of friends to try out Blue Apron, a company that sends ready-to-cook meals right to people's doors. Plenty of Betsy's friends have enjoyed the service and signed on for themselves. Betsy receives a reward from Blue Apron every time somebody signs up.

Another way to offer a reward is to start an affiliate program. You can offer your customers a 10 percent commission on the orders they bring to you. This system has generated millions of dollars for thousands of companies. A good affiliate program can do the work of an expensive sales force if you structure the percentages well.

Automate the Work

The easiest, fastest referral system can be automated using Mail Chimp, Infusionsoft, HubSpot, or any other e-mail marketing system. Simply include any customer who places one or two orders in an automated campaign that offers them an educational video or PDF they can pass on, an added value for telling their friends about you, or a bonus or even a commission. Make sure the system opts customers out after placing several orders so you don't hit every customer every time they order with another sales pitch. We don't want to risk annoying people.

SOME REAL-WORLD REFERRAL SYSTEMS

Implementing a referral system takes work, but it's effective. Take some inspiration from these samples. You'll quickly see that the effort will pay off.

A 100 Percent Refund for Three New Referrals Within a Semester. This was the brainchild of an after-school test-prep academy that prepared high school students for the SAT and ACT college admissions test, but it could just as well have been an eye doctor or a massage therapist. Parents were given a referral card to hand out to friends, many of whom had kids around the same age. Each time one of the cards came back, the referrer was credited hundreds of dollars because these courses were expensive! When they referred three new registrants, the referrer was given a 100 percent refund. Sure, the kids were competing with test scores, but the parents ended up competing for referrals, and business skyrocketed. The business also offered special seminars for parents and students of the 100 Percent Referral Club.

Invite-a-Friend Coupons. When students signed up for golf lessons, the range offered each new student several coupons for a free bucket of golf balls for a friend. While it's an individual game, golf is a social sport since people enjoy playing together. The course experienced a 40 percent increase in students signing up for lessons because word of mouth spread so effectively.

Open-House Party. Whenever a home contractor finished a large-scale project, he asked the homeowners if they would be willing to throw an open-house party in exchange for a slight discount. Friends, family, and neighbors were invited to a cookout on the newly built deck. The contractor used this opportunity to explain how the work was done and pass out cards. With only a few open-house parties, the contractor filled his schedule for the following twelve months.

Free Follow-Up Photos. A wedding photographer in Syracuse, New York, offered couples a free follow-up portrait on their one-year anniversary if the couple provided three referrals at the time of the wedding. She also followed up with cards to the entire bridal party, expressing how much of a pleasure it was to photograph them. Needless to say, business boomed because people who are in wedding parties often end up getting married soon themselves.

WHAT'S YOUR MARKETING PLAN?

In my twenties I spent an entire year playing chess. Nearly every day I met a friend at a coffee shop and we'd go at it for a couple of hours. My skills improved, and I ended up winning more than half my matches until another friend started showing up. He beat me every time, usually within twenty moves.

The reason? I knew a lot about the philosophy of chess, but I didn't have what's referred to as an *opening*. Before sitting down to play, my more skilled opponent planned his first five moves. This opening strategy was critical to his success. Once I memorized a few openings of my own, I started to win again.

If the StoryBrand Framework is a foundation, the five marketing ideas that make up the StoryBrand Marketing Roadmap should serve as your opening. These five simple yet powerful tools have been used by countless businesses to increase their revenue.

Again, consider this roadmap a checklist. After you've created your StoryBrand BrandScript, get to work on each aspect of this roadmap and watch as your customers engage and your company grows.

To hire a StoryBrand Certified Guide to help you execute your StoryBrand Marketing Roadmap, visit www.clarifyyourmessage.com. Our directory can help you find a StoryBrand Certified Guide (marketing coach), StoryBrand Certified Copywriter, web designer, videographer, printer, or even a complete design agency. Stop wasting money on marketing that doesn't work. Hire somebody who knows how to craft a clear message.

StoryBrand does not take a percentage of sales from any of our certified agents.

AFTERWORD

Sadly, you don't have to look around long to realize that often the people who are communicating the clearest aren't necessarily the people with the best products or services, and they're often not the people who are best qualified to lead.

Our hope at StoryBrand is to help the people who actually do make the best products and services, and the people who really should be leading, find their voice. We want the good guys holding the microphone more than the bad guys, to put it simply. Why? Because if hardworking people like you invite their customers into a story that makes their lives better, the world itself will become a better place.

Business is one of the most powerful forces in the world for good. With our businesses we provide jobs, a nine-to-five community for our teams, meaningful work for terrific people, and most importantly, products and services that solve our customers' problems.

There's a popular notion among cynics and politicians these days that says business is bad, that corporations are ruining the world. I suppose there are some bad eggs out there, but I've not met them. The clients we work with just want to improve their customers' lives, and I'm grateful to help them do so.

Getting up every day to grow your company is difficult work. I know how it feels to lose sleep wondering how you're going to make the bottom line so you don't have to let anybody go. The StoryBrand Framework was created to reduce this stress. It was created so you would be heard in the marketplace, grow your business, and transform your customers' lives. I'm grateful for the work you're doing. Your work is important.

It's true: if you confuse, you'll lose. But if you clarify your message, customers will listen. Here's to helping the good guys win.

Because in a good story, they always do.

ACKNOWLEDGMENTS

I'm grateful to Tim Schurrer, Kyle Reid, Koula Callahan, Avery Csorba, JJ Peterson, Chad Snavely, Suzanne Norman, Matt Harris, Brandon Dickerson, Tim Arnold, Matt Olthoff, and Betsy Miller for helping me build StoryBrand. Their tireless work on behalf of our clients has helped thousands of businesses connect with customers, hire more people, and solve their customers' problems. This team is more than a staff; they are family.

I'm also grateful to Mike Kim, who helped me edit this book into shape. Mike spent weeks going through the book making it better on every page. Webster Younce, Heather Skelton, and Brigitta Nortker of HarperCollins also contributed significantly to the book with their careful edits and additions.

Special thanks to Brandon Dickerson for his help fleshing out commercial evidence for the framework. Ben Ortlip lent invaluable feedback on how to implement the StoryBrand Framework in large organizations. I'm grateful for his help in creating our StoryBrand culture program along with his contribution to chapter 13. Ben's ability to take large corporations through a multifaceted program, allowing them to conquer the narrative void and see bottom-line results, has inspired us all.

Lastly, thank you. Thank you for daring to make and sell things, for solving customers' problems, helping heroes find homes, and putting your customers' stories above your own. As I said in the beginning, may you be richly rewarded for your effort.

PRAISE FOR THE STORYBRAND FRAMEWORK

"Before StoryBrand, customers weren't seeing themselves in our offering. We're a staffing agency that specializes in helping companies find and hire the right people. We help companies post job applications, we test candidates, and we provide software for applicant tracking. Sadly, our message, though, was all about us. We were talking about our strengths rather than the customer's needs. Also, our marketing material was too complex and hard to understand. After bringing in a StoryBrand facilitator, we clarified our message and made it about our customer. We revised our sales process and started listening to our customers' needs, asking them about their external problems and how those problems were making them feel in their daily work. The results were immediate. We created our BrandScript in December and spent the next couple months executing our new messaging across every part of the customer journey. Within seven months we'd seen a 118 percent increase in overall revenue. Yes, that means we more than doubled sales. We also saw a 276 percent increase in the number of paying customers during that same time period. And we're still growing. In the last six months, we've been increasing revenue 9 percent month over month, which really adds up!"

—Edwin Jansen, head of marketing, Fitzii

"Lipscomb University is one of the fastest growing universities in the Southeast, so it was no small task to get all the stories of our school clear and on mission. We knew it was important, and so we brought in StoryBrand to deliver a workshop to our entire faculty. Without question, it helped us understand who we were, who we were serving, and what we needed to communicate to offer value. After StoryBrand, each department felt like they were a subplot in the greater story of Lipscomb. The most tangible way we saw results was through our outreach to the community. We stopped positioning ourselves as the hero and instead began to serve the greater collective vision of Nashville. All of this culminated in a series called 'Imagine,' in which we brought in the mayor of Nashville, Governor Bill Haslam, and former president George W. Bush to speak about how Nashville and Lipscomb could positively contribute to the world. We stopped talking about us and we started serving as a guide to the community around us. Since this dramatic pivot, the renewed energy around a greater vision in which Lipscomb would play a part has resulted in more than $50 million in donations that will go toward development. I'd say the results have been fantastic."

—JOHN LOWRY, VICE PRESIDENT OF
DEVELOPMENT, LIPSCOMB UNIVERSITY

"Before StoryBrand, we at Reed's Dairy thought we had to tell people about us. Our marketing was clumsy and awkward, and our conversion rates on e-mails were declining. This was keeping me up at night. I bought the StoryBrand online course and put the framework to use immediately. We have an annual campaign in which we sell little milk coupons so people can buy their milk in advance, twenty gallons at a time. The most we'd ever sold through an e-mail campaign was $3,000 worth. We only do this campaign for one day each year, so we considered $3,000 pretty good. I wondered if the StoryBrand Framework could help us do even better. I sat and wrote that year's e-mail using a few of the things I had learned in the workshop. The response was incredible: $52,000 worth of coupon books in one day.

We'd never seen anything like it. I got on a plane to Nashville to attend the next live workshop and have since bought the copywriting course. Our conversion rates on our e-mails have more than doubled. In the last few months we've increased our extra product sales by 12.5 percent. We keep seeing results in everything we apply the framework to, including our retail stores and our ice cream division. I sleep pretty good these days."

—ALAN REED, CEO OF REED'S DAIRY

"I was asked to give a TED Talk about the work I do advocating for proton therapy as a treatment for cancer. As I reviewed the enormous binder of material I wanted to cover, I realized the task was epic. There was no way I could boil down all I wanted to say into an eighteen-minute talk. After spending a single day with a StoryBrand facilitator, I had hope. We mapped out my talk on a whiteboard, and I agreed to leave most of the things I wanted to talk about on the editing room floor. The talk was easy to memorize, flowed like a short story, and engaged the audience from beginning to end. StoryBrand didn't just help me prepare my TED Talk, they helped me understand how to better approach the advocacy I'd been doing. It all comes down to simple, repeatable messages that grab the audience. Without StoryBrand, I'd have never been able to clarify my message and inform the audience about a cause I care so deeply about. With the help of StoryBrand, I hit a home run, or more appropriately, I landed a triple luxe."

—SCOTT HAMILTON, OLYMPIC GOLD MEDALIST, FOUNDER
OF SCOTT CARES, AND THREE-TIME CANCER SURVIVOR

"These Numbers Have Faces is a nonprofit working to provide educational equality in Sub-Saharan Africa, where only 5 percent of the population will attend university. Before StoryBrand, our biggest problem was we were playing the hero. We talked more about our nonprofit than we did about our students or our donors. When we did talk about our students' problems, we talked about their external problems rather than their internal problems, which we now know is a limited way of approaching our messaging. After attending the StoryBrand workshop, we overhauled our messaging. In our e-mails, we began to connect donors with the narrative of the mission, and on social media, we told the stories of our heroic students. We used our StoryBrand BrandScript to draft our end-of-year report that got significant attention. As of today, we are on track to raise more money this year than ever before. We blew our fund-raising goal out of the water. We will go into next year with the largest cash advantage we've ever had. Team, donor, and student morale is at an all-time high."

—Justin Zoradi, executive director
of These Numbers Have Faces

"When EntreLeadership grew from a brand that basically just offered live events into a full-fledged coaching service for small business owners, we started experiencing challenges in how to explain what we did and how we did it. Even though we'd been writing copy and updating our website for years, the reality was that most of the time we were just guessing at the best way to say things. As a result people didn't understand our coaching service the way we thought they did. This was frustrating because the value of our program was so obvious to us. The mistake we made was assuming it was obvious to our customers too. We were clear . . . they were confused. That doesn't sell. I knew we were capable of more conversions and more effective connection with our audience, but I wasn't sure how to get there. It wasn't until we brought in a StoryBrand facilitator and sat down as a team to overhaul our entire world through the lens of the StoryBrand Framework that we became crystal clear on how to explain our coaching service. EntreLeadership has grown significantly, and we are tracking to more than double membership in the next two years. The StoryBrand Framework is an invaluable resource, and I now expect our marketers to use it in everything we create."

—Daniel Tardy, vice president of
EntreLeadership, Ramsey Solutions

"At Marie Mae we sell beautiful paper products and office supplies. Before StoryBrand, our marketing efforts were a jumbled mess. I once overheard a close friend talking about Marie Mae Company . . . and it was nothing close to what we were doing. I attended a StoryBrand Marketing Workshop and learned we were talking about the wrong things in our marketing copy. This was life changing for our start-up. We used the framework to simplify our message down to a single tagline: 'You are changing the world from your desk. Shouldn't your office products do the same?' We started focusing more on the meaningful work our customers were doing and showing how they could make an even bigger impact around the world just by choosing office products that also make an impact. We simplified our website using the SB7 Framework, and all of our marketing e-mails are now run through the SB7 filter as well. In the year since we implemented the StoryBrand Framework, we have increased our revenue by 20x and gotten our products into the hands of 250,000 people. We attribute this success largely to the clarity in our story and the shift in our marketing messages. We are grateful."

—JILLIAN RYAN, FOUNDER OF MARIE MAE COMPANY

"Before StoryBrand, I felt like my marketing was falling flat. I felt like my business had hit a ceiling. Going through the framework taught me I was talking about my programs all wrong. I used the StoryBrand Framework to recreate my sales material from scratch. It took quite a bit of effort to rethink the whole thing. I dipped my toes in the water by making a few changes to key pieces of marketing material, being sure they spoke directly to my clients' needs. I relaunched my program with my new sales materials and saw a massive response. A campaign that would have typically brought in $6,000 to $9,000 brought in more than $40,000. StoryBrand is the most practical, applicable, implementable, logical, simple, useful marketing program I've ever experienced. It's going to change everything in my business, and I'm just getting started."

—JENNY SHIH, BUSINESS COACH

"We often got a great deal of confusion when we tried to answer the question, 'So what do you *do?*' We were regularly frustrated by the fact that we had a huge body of organizational knowledge about our own work, and it required at least an hour to convey it to people. As a start-up, nonprofit organization, our revenue (donations) were barely enough to keep us afloat. We knew a big reason for this was that our model was a bit complex and it didn't get communicated with clarity, leaving potential donors confused. We took a big risk and chose to send our entire US team (three people) to StoryBrand—a risk that ate up a significant cut of our cash on hand. StoryBrand was indispensable for us. In the days following StoryBrand, we made a hard pivot on our communications strategy. Over the course of a couple months, we went from an organization on the verge of collapse to an organization that was thriving. In Q4 alone (post-StoryBrand), we literally tripled our annual revenue. Now Mavuno has expanded its reach by 400 percent in eastern Congo, and we are ending extreme poverty for thousands of Congolese. We are making dramatic change for some of the most vulnerable people in one of the world's most war-torn environments. We are postured for enormous scale, and that is due in large part to StoryBrand. Thank you for helping us change the world."

—Daniel Myatt, CEO of Mavuno

STORYBRAND RESOURCES

THE STORYBRAND ONLINE MARKETING WORKSHOP

If you learn better via video and would like to take an SB7 course on your own time and at your own pace, the StoryBrand Online Marketing Workshop walks you through the creation of your BrandScript while giving plenty of examples and inspirational stories of success. Once you're done with the course, you will have a message you can use to create websites, keynotes, elevator pitches, and much more. Get the course at storybrand.com/online.

STORYBRAND MARKETING ROADMAP ONLINE COURSE (A COURSE IN COPYWRITING)

Donald Miller and copywriting legend Ray Edwards team up to teach you how to write a great sales letter, wireframe a website, create a one-liner, write an e-mail campaign, and much more. If you want to learn to write terrific sales copy using the StoryBrand method, then get the course at storybrand.com/roadmap.

THE STORYBRAND LIVE MARKETING WORKSHOP

If you want to get away and clarify your message while being surrounded by exciting peers who are also working to grow their companies, sign up for our live workshop. Our facilitators will show you endless examples of successful messaging and coach you to make sure you're creating the perfect BrandScript for your company. Not only this, but we will review best practices in simple marketing techniques that will give you a plan moving forward. Get away for two days and walk away with the entire process this book describes finished and ready for execution. Our live workshops will get you results. Register for a workshop today at storybrand.com.

THE STORYBRAND PRIVATE WORKSHOP

Walking your people through the StoryBrand Framework in the comfort of your own office is the next step to aligning your team, growing your business, reducing marketing costs, and creating a common language that excites and inspires your team. You'll spend two days clarifying your StoryBrand BrandScript and unifying your team, and our facilitators will even take a look at your existing marketing materials once your BrandScript is created. The private workshop process takes 1.5 days, and your company will never be the same. Get more information at storybrand.com/privateworkshop.

BECOME A CERTIFIED STORYBRAND GUIDE

If you'd like to give great marketing advice by helping people clarify their message and execute the StoryBrand Marketing Roadmap, apply to become a Certified StoryBrand Guide. StoryBrand Guides are approved through an interview process and then listed in our online directory. Those who have a knack for marketing and messaging and want to start a coaching business, along with existing coaches looking to increase their value, are welcome to apply. Corporations wanting to certify members of their team may also apply. You can learn more at storybrand.com/guide.

STORYBRAND COPYWRITER CERTIFICATION

StoryBrand clients often need a copywriter, and if you want to be one of them, you have to do more than just take the online course; you have to be certified. Donald Miller and Ray Edwards have teamed up to create a robust certification course that will equip you to write copy that gets results. As a StoryBrand Certified Copywriter, you will understand how to wireframe a website, create a one-liner, write an e-mail campaign, draft a terrific sales letter, and more. And once you're certified, you'll be listed on our website so potential customers can find you. Only a select number of copywriters are certified each year. Certification can be done online through our courses and an assessment. Register at storybrand.com/copywriter.

STORYBRAND AGENCY CERTIFICATION

If you have a design agency and want to use the SB7 Framework to create marketing collateral for your clients, you can be listed in our Agency Certification database by taking our agency certification program. Each program is custom-comprised for each agency based on how many designers, copywriters, and project managers your team includes. Find out more at storybrand.com/agency.

STORYBRAND CULTURE PROGRAM

Large companies are more fractured than ever. As a company grows and succeeds, the plot often starts to get lost. Our culture program helps a large corporation create an overall StoryBrand BrandScript, create a BrandScript for each division, create onboarding curriculum to implement the BrandScript company-wide, and create a custom plan to radically affect the *thoughtmosphere* of your organization. Our culture program works with individual companies to create custom strategies to make sure your entire team is on the same page, acting as a unified body, and moving forward toward your mission. If your team members don't fully understand the story you're inviting customers into, schedule a culture analysis today. Schedule your analysis at storybrand.com/culture.

STORYBRAND TRAIN THE TRAINER

Do you want to teach your entire team to clearly communicate the value your brand offers? If you want to convert your sales team, marketing team, managers, and executive leadership into Guides that serve their hero customers, have your facilitators trained by StoryBrand. We will train your facilitators to train your people. Find out more at StoryBrand.com/corporate.

NOTES

Chapter 2: The Secret Weapon That Will Grow Your Business

1. Samantha Sharf, "The World's Largest Tech Companies 2016: Apple Bests Samsung, Microsoft and Alphabet," Forbes.com, May 26, 2016, http://www.forbes.com/sites/samanthasharf/2016/05/26/the-worlds-largest-tech-companies-2016-apple-bests-samsung-microsoft-and-alphabet/#2b0c584d89ee.
2. Alfred Hitchcock: Quotes, IMDB, http://m.imdb.com/name/nm0000033/quotes.

Chapter 3: The Simple SB7 Framework

1. "Great Presentations: Understand the Audience's Power," *Duarte*, http://www.duarte.com/great-presentations-understand-the-audiences-power/.
2. Ronald Reagan, "Farewell Address to the Nation," January 11,

1989, The American Presidency Project, http://www.presidency
.ucsb.edu/ws?pid+29650.

3. "President Bill Clinton—Acceptance Speech," *PBS Newshour*, August 29, 1996, http://www.pbs.org/newshour/bb/ politics-july-dec96-clinton_08-29/.

4. Claire Suddath, "A Brief History of Campaign Songs: Franklin D. Roosevelt," *Time*, http://content.time.com/time/specials/ packages/article/0,28804,1840998_1840901,00.html.

Chapter 4: A Character

1. Viktor E. Frankl, *Man's Search for Meaning* (Boston: Beacon Press, 2006).

Chapter 5: Has a Problem

1. James Scott Bell, *Plot & Structure: Techniques and Exercises for Crafting a Plot That Grips Readers from Start to Finish* (Cincinnati, OH: Writer's Digest Books, 2004), 12.

2. "Why CarMax?," CarMax.com, accessed February 10, 2017, https://www.carmax.com/car-buying-process/why-carmax.

3. "The Just 100: America's Best Corporate Citizens," *Forbes*, May 2016, http://www.forbes.com/companies/carmax/.

Chapter 6: And Meets a Guide

1. James Scott Bell, *Plot & Structure: Techniques and Exercises for Crafting a Plot That Grips Readers from Start to Finish* (Cincinnati, OH: Writer's Digest Books, 2004), 31–32.

2. Christopher Booker, *The Seven Basic Plots: Why We Tell Stories* (London: Continuum, 2004), 194.

3. Ben Sisario, "Jay Z Reveals Plans for Tidal, a Streaming Music Service," *New York Times*, March 30, 2015, https://www .nytimes.com/2015/03/31/business/media/jay-z-reveals-plans -for-tidal-a-streaming-music-service.html.

4. Ibid.

5. "Clinton vs. Bush in 1992 Debate," YouTube video, 4:08, posted

by "Seth Masket," March 19, 2007, https://www.youtube.com/watch?v=7ffbFvK1WqE.

6. Infusionsoft home page, accessed February 9, 2017, https://www.infusionsoft.com.

7. Amy Cuddy, *Presence: Bringing Your Boldest Self to Your Biggest Challenges* (New York: Little Brown and Company, 2015), 71–72.

Chapter 7: Who Gives Them a Plan

1. "Why CarMax?," CarMax.com, accessed February 10, 2017, https://www.carmax.com/car-buying-process/why-carmax.

2. Arlena Sawyers, "Hot Topics, Trends to Watch in 2016," *Automotive News*, December 28, 2015, http://www.autonews.com/article/20151228/RETAIL04/312289987/hot-topics-trends-to-watch-in-2016.

Chapter 9: That Helps Them Avoid Failure

1. Susanna Kim, "Allstate's 'Mayhem' Is Biggest Winner of College Bowl," ABC News, January 2, 2015, http://abcnews.go.com/Business/allstates-mayhem-biggest-winner-college-bowl/story?id=27960362.

2. Daniel Kahneman and Amos Tversky, "Prospect Theory: An Analysis of Decision under Risk" (*Econometrica, 47(2)*, March 1979), 263–91, https://www.princeton.edu/~kahneman/docs/Publications/prospect_theory.pdf.

3. Dominic Infante, Andrew Rancer, and Deanna Womack, *Building Communication Theory* (Long Grove, IL: Waveland Press, 2003), 149.

4. Ibid., 150.

Chapter 10: And Ends in a Success

1. Stew Friedman, "The Most Compelling Leadership Vision," *Harvard Business Review*, May 8, 2009, https://hbr.org/2009/05/the-most-compelling-leadership.

Chapter 11: People Want Your Brand to Participate in Their Transformation

1. "Hello Trouble," Vimeo video, 1:44, posted by Adam Long, February 13, 2013, https://vimeo.com/59589229.

Chapter 13: Using StoryBrand to Transform Company Culture

1. The Gallup Organizaion (1992-1999). Gallup Workplace Audit, Washington, DC: U.S. Copyright Office.

2. Susan Sorenson and Keri Garman, "How to Tackle U.S. Employees' Stagnating Engagement," Gallup, June 11, 2013, http://www.gallup.com/businessjournal/162953/tackle-employees-stagnating-engagement.aspx.